THE 11 ELEMENTS
OF PRUDENT INVESTING

THE 11 ELEMENTS OF PRUDENT INVESTING

Andy Karabinos

Writers Advantage

San Jose New York Lincoln Shanghai

The 11 Elements of Prudent Investing

Writers Advantage
an imprint of iUniverse, Inc.

For information address:
iUniverse, Inc.
5220 S. 16th St., Suite 200
Lincoln, NE 68512
www.iuniverse.com

Always perform due dilligence on your investments.
If it doesn't make sense, don't do it!

ISBN: 0-595-23423-2

Printed in the United States of America

In Memory of

Mary and Andy Karabinos, my parents, who provided the basis for this book,

And Mary Karabinos, my wife, who taught me the true value of living.

CONTENTS

PREFACE

Those who are expecting to find within these pages a "Holy Grail" or magic formula to make money through investing will be sadly disappointed. In accordance with the philosophy established by Sun Tzu in his *Art of War*, written 2500 years ago, (repeated by an untold number of authors since), "There first must be developed a successful philosophy of combat." This philosophy, combined with experience, will help determine opportunities, which a flexible operator can exploit to his advantage. It can be summarized best as the fine art of being prepared to reduce risk and enhance rewards. There is more to investing than looking at a balance sheet. It is the intention of this book to delve into the entire processes behind successful investing.

Many years ago, when I was still a child, my father and mother shared with me their investment activities. They began investing in the stock market in the mid-1930s after accumulating a few dollars from their grocery store. The Great Depression was very trying, and success was realized only by the prudent investor. From them I learned many lessons of value.

In the early 1950s I saved money and began investing using their accounts with my money. By 1954, I had my own broker account using small amounts of money. My first "big" investment was thirty shares of American Motors at $3 a share. Using my dad's philosophy and a few years' time, the $100 investment grew to more than $1000. I performed research at public libraries or at the broker's office. The family duties involved with a wife and seven children left little time for investing.

By 1987, I had a self-directed Individual Retirement Account (IRA), which combined with my regular portfolio provided a nice six-figure nest egg. The high volatility of that period motivated me to assume a less risky investment posture. Following the advice of my broker, I invested heavily in LTV convertible debentures, which were highly discounted and paying high interest rates. When the company went bankrupt six months later, I lost about 95 percent of my entire portfolio, including the IRA. Combined with the crash of October 1987, my total retirement nest egg would barely buy a mid-priced used car.

At the first opportunity after shock recovery, I revisited my father. At that point in time and with his help, I began recording the important elements of investing which resulted in this document. I realized the failure was not the fault of my broker, but my violation of prudent investing practices. I knew better. As time progressed I added to this base of knowledge from an uncountable number of sources.

Within six years, the investment account had recovered, but the reader should know that the lessons presented herein were purchased at a very high cost. Few (if any) of the concepts presented are original, but each is time tested and true.

Some time ago, I decided to write down these lessons to give to my children. After some expansions, I used this knowledge to assist my friends in investing. Eventually, as a member and past president of the Huntsville PC User's Group, I formed a special interest group, called Computer Aided Investing, to help members use computers to enhance their investing skills.

Certain senior groups became interested and the number of requests grew to a point where it seemed prudent to publish this document. It was prepared to provide the most information, using the least number of words and pages, thereby requiring the least time (and effort) to read. However, it is not light reading and will need to be studied. Also the reader will note many subjects are touched on lightly and any interested reader will need to do more research on his own.

This document is intended to allow the less experienced investor to understand the elements of prudent investing in the minimum amount of time, and to see the basic essentials of how the markets operate in relation to other types of investments. It presents other factors that may affect your investment. The large majority of examples will deal with stocks, try to answer some of the anticipated questions of beginners, and teach some of the language and concepts of investing and trading.

The eleven elements are divided into three groups. The first group of three elements is useful to everybody who has ever saved any money. These elements are:

Common Sense

Responsibilities

Strategies.

The second group of four elements is useful to either active or passive investors. They are:

Quality of Information

Legends of Wall Street

Gurus

Quality of Company Management

The third group of four analytical elements is most useful to active investors. They are:

Fundamental Analysis

Technical Analysis

Macroeconomics

Market Forces.

The prudent investor will consider all of these elements in the process of making any investment decision. All are not equally applicable, and all do not require the same expenditure of time and effort. However, all of them can significantly reduce risk and promote success. Ignore them at your peril.

Of great importance is understanding their application so that you may evaluate the efforts of the person(s) managing your investments. The ultimate goal is to develop a productive "teddy bear" portfolio. That is the kind you can sleep with at night.

Assume one or more of the following happened to you: 1) Your rich uncle died and left you a small (or large) fortune; 2) You had an accident and the insurance company awarded you a substantial amount of money; 3) You received a lump sum of money as part of your retirement program; 4) You had been making payments on a house for several years, and when you sold it, you had a large equity that you should invest; and 5) You just saved some money and want to put it to work. For the first time you are confronted with the responsibility of investing some money. What should you do?

First, don't screw up!!

ACKNOWLEDGMENTS

I am grateful for the assistance of Don and Patti Wilson, Barbara Atchley, Al Norman, members of the Huntsville PC User's Group, the Senior Center, the UAH Academy of Lifetime Learning, the teachings of Don Worden of the TC-2000 service, my many friends and neighbors, public programs like Louis Rukeyser's Wall Street Week, CNBC, and uncountable others. When I started to accumulate this information several decades ago, I never planned to publish anything, and therefore did not keep a list of sources. With the advent of senior memory lapses, I have no way to determine the source of a specific piece of information. If I miss giving a credit, I am sorry.

First Element—Common Sense

One of the first impulses is to enlist the services of somebody who is reputed to "know a lot" and have them tell you what to do. This is particularly true of widows whose husbands have passed away, when he always took care of all the financial problems. Many people will go to a banker or broker and tell them to invest the money.

To do this it is necessary to find someone who is trustworthy and will have your interests at heart. Unfortunately, crooks are just as charming as the good guys, and will not appear to be crooks. It is difficult to determine if the person you select is being truthful. The solution to this problem is to learn at least enough about the elements of investing to evaluate their proposal and make a good assessment of their capabilities.

The first and foremost element is common sense and this is the time to use it. Common sense is acquired through experience. You may not have "been there, done that" but you've seen that type of thinking before, and recognize the risk involved. Common sense is your biggest weapon against losing money. It is surprising how many sophisticated investors do not take the time to look over a situation and fall for a sales pitch that is "too good to be true." First and most importantly, if you feel uncomfortable with the presentation, don't do anything!

For example: somebody comes to you who knows somebody (out of the country) who has several millions of dollars and wants to sneak it out of the country. He will give you half if you give him your savings account number and authorization to take out his half when it is transferred into your account. Only someone very greedy and naïve or without any financial knowledge will even consider that offer. The huge majority of people will not fall for that scam. However, the real scam is to sell this scheme to

1

some person in a foreign country, making that person think he will make a lot of money scamming other people here. It is very hard to cheat an honest man.

The greatest and most often used ploy is to present a complicated investment scheme and expect you to make a conclusion in a very short period of time. When you ask questions, they imply that you are not very smart if you don't understand this investment procedure. It's a good rule of thumb that if they can't explain it clearly and in layman's terms, then they either don't know it, or do not want you to know it.

Common sense begs you to believe that if they can't explain it clearly, then consider it a scam. The emotions of greed (I can make a lot of money with no effort or risk) and fear (If I don't accept soon I'll will lose this fortune) are the enemy of common sense. Avoiding these twin evils may cause you to miss a few good investments over a lifetime, but will also permit you to save a lot of money. This common sense needs to be applied equally to the buying and selling of investments. The other elements described below will help with the financial knowledge, but you will always need to use common sense.

SECOND ELEMENT—RESPONSIBILITY

Be assured there will be a lot of advice, much of it from people who have little or no experience in these matters and have no responsibility for your success. It is well advised to remember that **it is your responsibility** to look after your money. Many people prefer to take their money and put it into the hands of someone "smarter" who knows how to invest wisely. There are three problems. First, how do you know he is really smarter than you are? Second, how do you tell that person what you really want (or need)? And third, how do you tell when/if he's doing what you wanted him to do?

It is essential for you to take a little time to figure out how much risk you can tolerate (consider risk as the amount of money you can afford to lose), and find out how much reward that will produce. It is up to you to establish the criteria by which your money is to be managed. If that takes some study on your part, then **it is your responsibility** to do that study. That does not mean you have to be an expert. But it does mean you have to learn the rules of the road. You do have to spend some time learning about investing. Complaining that you have selected a poor advisor or that you did not give him the correct information is usually fruitless. This document is intended to provide you with information and a start along the process of learning about investing.

Investment Paths

The investor may decide to have someone help invest the money. But you should have enough knowledge to be able to look over their shoulder and determine if they are doing what you want and to change it if they are not. A broker or banker is not endowed with the ability to read a person's mind. Without guidance, they will usually put you in an investment that will not cause them problems and that can earn the most with a minimum amount of (their) work. They usually make their living on commissions. As a result they must spend their time in proportion to the size of the portfolio. The best approach from the broker's view is usually to create a low risk–low reward portfolio.

There are two basic investment paths. The first is debt instruments. That is where you loan some of your money to someone else and they pay you interest for the loan. At certain fixed times they will pay you back the interest and principal. You do not own any part of the property. A bank does this when you make a loan on your house. Examples include bonds, certificate of deposits (CDs), savings accounts, and promissory notes.

The second path is called equity investments. Here you own a part or an entire investment. An example is a house, stocks, partnerships, and property you rent to others for profit. If the property goes up or down in price, you benefit or cry, whichever is appropriate. Large companies may sell stock when they are formed, and the stockholders own the company. These companies pay a part of the earnings as dividends (instead of interest) to the stockholders as a reward of ownership. They may also pay interest to bond-holders who do not own any part of the company, but own a lien against the company. But only the stockholders share in the profits. A successful well-managed company will grow over time. Over 90 percent of all jobs in the U.S. are with such companies. The size ranges from a one-man operation to companies whose stock is worth a half trillion dollars (1999). The major benefit to the stockholders is the appreciation of price over time. **It is your responsibility** to decide how much of your portfolio is invested in each path.

Where to Put My Money

Another decision the investor needs to make concerns the level of his or her participation. This level depends on how much time one can (or is willing to) spend on managing the money, and the amount of risk one is willing to tolerate. Some people completely manage their investments, but usually it's a sharing process in which another person or institution is help-ing. Divide the problem into three categories based on the sharing arrangement:

The first category includes the person who wants to spend a minimal amount of time and effort. This should be no less than one hour a month in all cases. That person should have a full-service broker or banker to make most or all of the decisions, and the primary effort on the part of the investor should be spent checking up on the broker or banker's perform-ance. This should be done at least once a month, and the time is devoted to comparing your investment to the average of similar investments. For exam-ple, if the investment is in stocks with a broker, then compare your portfolio to the Standard & Poor's 500 or the Dow Jones Industrial Average. If the investment is in CDs with a banker, then compare to the national average interest rate with that holding term. The object is to avoid the banker put-ting you in a savings account at 2 percent interest when you could be put-ting the majority in a CD at 7 percent and a small amount in a money market checking account at 4 percent. It does happen. The process of some-one else making the investing decisions is called "passive" investing.

The second category includes a person who can spend between one hour a month and six hours a week. This person should be more involved in selecting the investments, and is with either a full-service broker or a discount broker, depending on the level of experience. A full-service bro-ker will give investment advice from their research department and keep the investor from making drastic errors. The discount broker does not do research, but will (usually) prevent the person from a catastrophic mistake. The discount broker charges lower fees and may be on the internet. This person will invest mostly in funds, and some selected low-risk stocks. This is active investing, but at a minimal level.

If he has a full-service broker, he may sell covered call options (options are financial derivatives of other investments, usually stocks). On occasion, some investors lie to the discount or online broker about their experience, and get in over their heads. Some time ago that happened to a day trader in Atlanta who went on a shooting spree after he was wiped out in the market. It is advised that a broker be used when experimenting with new investing techniques. All brokers require an investor to fill out a form to define his level of experience and will prevent him from trading in areas in which he has inadequate experience. Working with a good broker is the best way to gain experience

The third category is the very active investor, a person who has the experience and is willing to spend from two to fifty hours per week. But most important, he enjoys the study of financial markets and the economy. People never get good at something they do not like. If you do **not** like doing this, you will lose money. If this type of investor wants to take a month's vacation and be totally away from the market, he can put his portfolio in a "safe" mode for that period of time.

Usually this person takes higher risks, receives higher rewards, trades online, has developed a profitable strategy, is well disciplined, and spends most of his time doing research either on the Internet or reading newspapers and magazines. **The most effective method of reducing risk is with added knowledge.** He may invest or trade in stocks, derivatives, commodities, and futures. He will seldom, if ever, "take a chance" or commit his money "just to see what will happen." All of his financial commitments are well planned.

Included in the third category are professional or semi-professionals who make a living trading stocks. These are not really long-term investors but are traders who use sophisticated technical analysis to determine the direction and momentum of various stocks. There are enough of them so that their presence can be felt. They tend to seek out weaknesses in a stock, and by the use of short selling (see Glossary), can increase the level of volatility of a stock substantially. They tend to make extra money from the panic selling caused by the aforementioned greed and fear.

Some less experienced traders use an advisory service to help them trade stocks. These services do the analysis, and the trader can accomplish a similar effect with less analytical skills. In a rising market these traders can sometimes produce handsome profits, but are quite vulnerable in a changing market. If the advisory service is wrong, the trader sinks

Finally, some investors, called day traders, are considered arbitrageurs and act as in-between buyers and sellers of stocks and provide liquidity to the market. They generally make their money on the difference between the bid and asked price. This requires a fast system; the day trader may make one hundred trades a day, have a minimum of $100,000 at risk, and spend eight hours per day on his investments. This is a job. Day traders also have a different income tax status.

All of the above estimated time requirements do not include the time required to gain the needed level of expertise. That time will vary widely depending on age, education, and other experience. The scope of this book is directed to longer term investing and not trading. There are a myriad of good books on trading. The classic Bible of trading is *The Technical Analysis of Stock Trends* by Robert D. Edwards and John Magee.

Investing vs. Gambling

Often, people equate playing the stock market with gambling. The common expression "to bet on a stock" gives an inaccurate portrayal of investing. There is risk in investing, as there is also risk in crossing the street, riding in a car, or playing a slot machine. In investing, the probability is that the investor will make money; i.e., the odds favor the investor. In gambling, the probability is that the gambler will lose money. In a casino, the patron is gambling while the house is investing.

This is best demonstrated by looking at the ratio of risk to reward. Both risk and reward can be expressed in dollars. For prudent investing the object is for the reward to be larger than the risk. In gambling, the risk is always larger than the reward. If you play the nickel slots for a very long time, say 100,000 times, you will gain 97,000 nickels for each 100,000 nickels you put in, because the payout ratio is usually 97 percent. (The payout ratio is the amount received divided by the amount invested, including the original investment and differs with machines and times). For short times you can (and often will) be ahead, but in the long run, you will always lose. When someone else hits a jackpot, part of the money he gets is from your contribution. This is a high risk–low reward endeavor.

However, the stock market has returned a payout ratio of over 100 percent for any extended time period. If a person put $100 in the Dow Jones

Average on March 1, 1950, he would have $4978.88 by March 1, 2000. The total does not include dividends that were paid during that time. This is a profit compounded at the rate of 8.12 percent per year, or to compare with gambling, a payout ratio of over 108 percent. Please note, this doesn't mean you can't lose. It means the odds are in the investor's favor, and with a prudent attitude anyone can do well investing. In fact, the large majority of investors succeed in accumulating money. In that way, the reward is higher than the risk. But the investor is cautioned that **each stock will not necessarily perform as the average, and well may go down or fail during the investment period.**

The general belief is that the higher the risk, the higher the reward. Do not be fooled by that statement. The probability of collecting the reward must be figured into the equation. If it is a 100 to 1 shot and it happens only a few times in your lifetime, then the probability of the event actually occurring is too small. Consider a U.S. government bond. It may pay only 6 percent. You will risk $100 and receive a reward of $106 a year later. The probability based on past history is so near perfect that it can be considered 100 percent true, and you will most likely receive your 6 percent interest each year for the rest of your life.

Compare that to a loan to your drunken, out-of-work brother-in-law who only paid you back once in the last twenty years. Lend him $100 with a payback of $1000 (1000 percent) in sixty days, and the probability of actually collecting it is so low that you can consider it a gift. Or more appropriately, consider the lottery, which has a 50 percent payout. You risk $1, but the probability of winning the 5 million prize, against the 10 million people betting, is still 1 in 10 million. Your reward is fifty cents for each dollar risked. If you bet one dollar a week, you should win once in the next 192,307 years. But then again you may not.

Younger investors often take higher risks without commensurate rewards. High-quality corporate management is generally the lowest risk proposition. The secret of successful investing, if there is such a thing, is to find well-managed companies whose prices are out of proportion on the low side. We often call these oversold, bargain, or value stocks.

Below are some examples of typical (no bargains) risk / reward / gain / comparisons. All numbers are rough estimates. Risk is given as the probability of losing some or all of your original capital as well as the potential gain. Reward is given as the probability of keeping the original investment and the potential gain. The gain is the expected return on your investment (per year) expressed as a percent of your original investment. As the risk increases, not only does the probability of loss increase, but the confidence of the rewards being as shown diminishes. These numbers are my "gut" feelings; they are meant to give you an idea of where all of these items rank in relation to each other over long periods of time.

Item:	Probability of Risk (%):	Probability of Reward (%):	Projected Gain (%):
U.S. Government bonds and notes, CDs, bank accounts	Lowest 0.1	Highest 99.9	+2 to +7
Corporate bonds, mortgage paper, real estate, some bond funds	Low 1 to 10	High 90 to 95	+5 to +12
Blue chip stocks, funds, junk bonds, well-manages companies	Low 5 to 20	Medium 70 to 95	+8 to +40
Average companies, older businesses, poorly manages funds	Medium 10 to 40	Low to High 20 to 80	0 to +30
Initial public offerings, untested management, speculative companies	High 10 to 100	Low 5 to 20	-100 to +1000
Casino gambling	High 90 to 100	Low 0 to 3	-50 to -3

In the investment industry the primary measure of success is Return on Investment (ROI). Return on Investment is the amount of money you receive over and above the original investment. Sometimes it is also calculated as Return on Equity (ROE). If you borrowed some of the investment money, your return on equity would be calculated on that portion you own, which is called equity.

Risk analysis is usually determined by calculating the ratio of gain to loss. For example, if the investment went as planned and a reasonable expectation of gain is $3 and the potential loss is $1, the ratio would be 3 to 1. Then include the probability of success. The areas of interest include currency transactions, political problems, adverse government regulation, diplomatic problems, and technical problems, all of which increase costs or would have an adverse effect on profit potential.

A company with a high percentage of overseas operations and a volatile currency market would experience currency risk. Political risk would consider adverse economic reaction from party philosophy or a negative attitude toward profit-making companies. Regulation would include government (ours or others) controls of the price of service, such as with a utility company.

Diplomatic risk includes the political ramifications of the political philosophy of foreign governments. Technical risks are associated with the problem of making a profit from new and/or untried phenomena, like putting a man on the moon or advanced weapons technology. However, technical rewards are often the greatest because they are not associated with the severe emotions connected to political, diplomatic, and religious issues.

Considering the above, there are two basic approaches to your participation. First is passive investing, in which someone else makes the decisions and you monitor their success or failure. The second is active investing, in which you actually manage and make your own decisions, sometimes with the help of others.

Before you make the decision of which approach you will take, **it is prudent to make an honest and critical appraisal of your abilities.** This is where most people get into trouble. They either overestimate their ability to judge risk, (often men with technical backgrounds) or underestimate their ability to learn (often women with low self-confidence). Note: Women are generally more successful investors because they tend to take fewer risks. Higher risks are much more difficult to assess.

Either situation is easily overcome, but not without discipline and work. Let us define discipline as the ability to do what you need to do rather than what you want to do. With a good appraisal of yourself, you can make an appropriate decision with respect to objectives and risk.

To make a lot of money fast is not a good financial objective because to do that would require high risk as explained above. Younger investors would normally select higher growth and would be able to tolerate a medium amount of risk because if there were an adverse occurrence, they would have enough time for recovery before retirement. An older investor would normally select lower risk because there is not enough time left to overcome a substantial loss if it were to occur. The factors involved in developing financial objectives include: risk, time left before retirement, place in the economic cycle, amount, if any, of the portfolio needed to live on, and cost of lifestyle.

Passive Investments

Prudent investing requires a considerable level of interest and discipline. It is safe to say that not everyone is interested in or well-suited for performing this task unaided. These people have two options. The first is to seek a competent full-service stockbroker. The second is to invest in a mutual fund. A mutual fund is an organization that invests your money in stocks and bonds using professional money managers.

If you are interested in low- or ultra low-risk investments like government bonds, CDs and savings accounts, it is best to talk to someone in a national bank or credit union. They will have all of these and other similar financial products. Banking is a very regulated and controlled industry, which is the reason for the low risk. Anyone with a substantial amount of money should have already established a good banking relationship. The reward will generally be lower than equity investing.

If the investor wants to invest in equities and has little or no experience, he or she should enlist the services of a broker as mentioned above. Even with a broker, a prudent investor will need to spend some time each week reviewing his or her investments. With the advent of the Internet, there is no excuse for an individual to be uninformed.

An investor using a broker must realize that the broker's time is precious. Consider that a broker will probably need about $20 to $40 million in accounts to make a living. If you have $250,000 invested, then a broker can only spend about a half-hour per week on you. He cannot afford to spend much time trying to determine the best investments for you. Generally the broker's research department will provide a list of typical investments for people in your circumstances.

However, you will be a great deal more successful by doing a lot of the thinking yourself and providing the broker with information so he will know how to give you the best advice in the least possible time. Once both of you select a stock, you need to follow it because he may not have enough time. The alternative is that he will churn your stocks to develop more commissions, and no one is in favor of that.

If you are interested in doing some investigations but do not want to be very active, a mutual fund is a good avenue for investing. There are thousands of funds, and the Internet has several programs for evaluating and ranking all of them. A good place to start is http://quote.yahoo.com. There are stock and bond funds, including Index, large, small, mid-cap, growth, value, blend, balanced, and specialty funds. Also included are funds that specialize in communications, financials, health, natural resources, energy, precious metals, real estate, technology, and utilities. Others are international (some are country specific), and there are government tax-free municipals bond funds.

Some funds charge a load (sales commission) plus operating costs, while others include marketing costs as part of expenses. In theory load funds hire better managers and perform better than no load funds. Index funds have a very low operating expense because the portfolio is determined by the index and there is no need to hire professionals to pick the stocks. It is possible to see how these funds have performed over short and long periods of time, as well as a list of their top ten holdings. All larger funds have Web pages, and a plethora of information on each fund is available. Morningstar.com provides a service that evaluates and ranks funds by performance. This information is available over the Web or at most public libraries.

There is one feature of funds related to income taxes to be understood before investing in them. For most people, and all people with IRAs or 401Ks or tax-deferred portfolios, it does not make a difference. However, for those who invest in funds with taxable money, it is necessary to know funds must "pass through" all profits to the fund holder (pass through means the fund must send, by the end of the year, to the fund holder all the dividends and capital gains received, and retain none for the use of the fund). Otherwise severe tax consequences are encountered by the fund and this affects your investment. The fund must pass through its profits to avoid being taxed twice. What this means is that if you elect to reinvest all of your dividends, at the end of the year you may get a tax bill and no money because your money has been reinvested. For those prepared for this condition, it is not a problem, but others have found it to be an unpleasant surprise. It may happen that the individual has a substantial tax bill yet his portfolio is down.

But with well-managed equity funds, the risk is relatively low and rewards reasonable. Long-term gains have averaged in excess of 15 percent annually. A passive investor may not need to be proficient in all elements of investing, but he or she needs to apply common sense to determine if the investments are meeting the goals established by the investor without excessive risks, as expected by the preplanned strategy. Often, funds change portfolios over the years to match the success of competing funds, resulting in the fund managers taking unacceptable risks.

Active Investments

Real estate investments, that is, buying a property with the intention of renting it out, is a good investment. It is profitable and has a reasonably low risk; however, it suffers from lack of liquidity and requires a long-term commitment. Real estate is unique to each locality so it would be wise to establish a good relationship with a local real estate broker. This close relationship will allow the investor to learn more about the peculiarities of the local area and have the best chance of obtaining the best bargains. ROI is just as important here as with other investments. However, the stock market has Real Estate Investment Trusts (REITs), which are purchased as stocks, and hold rental real estate, (mostly commercial) in large cities. But REITs are more of a passive investment.

If you are well disciplined and have an interest in business affairs, you may be interested in making your own decisions by investing in equity or debt instruments via the stock market. There are three approaches to self-directed investing in equities. The first is to enlist the services of a licensed stockbroker. The second is to join an investment club sanctioned by the National Association of Investment Clubs (NAIC) or the American Association of Individual Investors (AAII). The third is to do all the research yourself, and trade through a discount broker or online.

Anyone intent on being an active investor needs to develop adequate acumen in all elements of investing. In order to properly appreciate the scope of this endeavor, carefully read the remaining nine elements of prudent investing. It is your responsibility.

THIRD ELEMENT—INVESTING STRATEGIES

Strategy: "A careful plan or method of accomplishing a given task. Achieving success by employing forces most efficiently." Usually this term is applied to activities associated with war or conflicts, and is subjective in nature because it is used comparatively without regard to absolute values. Other things being equal, the side with the best strategy will win. Or, as often recorded in wars, a superior strategy will compensate for inferior equipment or personnel.

In a family where strategy is applied to investing assets, it is best by far if both members contribute, understand, and are able to execute the investment strategy. Should a tragedy strike the family and one member die, whether young or retired, it is irrational to expect the remaining spouse who is not knowledgeable to begin an efficient learning process.

A good investment strategy will result in better portfolio performance, but more importantly it will produce lower risk. A strategy can be wide ranging to include investing over an entire lifetime or selective for shorter periods. But in all cases, a good strategy should include, but not be limited to, the following:

- It must be easy to understand by the portfolio owner.
- It must be adaptable and amenable to changing conditions.
- It must provide reasonably accurate assessment of risk and reward.
- It must not require constant tinkering.
- It must contain reasonable long- and short-term goals.
- It must be portable.

Please note the ultimate criterion of successful investing is the Return On Investment (ROI) for the time period involved. After we take a look at risk, we review several different types of strategies as shown below. The reader should be able to recognize one or more applicable to his or her particular situation.

Risk

As noted earlier, there are two important elements to financial risk. The first is the probability of loss, and the second is the estimate of the probable amount of the loss. In order to determine the most appropriate strategy, it is of paramount importance to develop an assessment of the associated risks that is as accurate as possible.

Consider investing in a company stock or bond. A stock is equity or shared ownership of the company, while a bond is a loan to the company to build a building, which will be used as collateral for the loan. If a catastrophe hits the company, and it is destroyed or goes out of business (say because of war), neither stock nor bond will pay as before. But the bond will have some value because the probability of getting something back is much better.

Of course, the risk (including both probabilities) must be compared with all the rewards to make a cogent investment decision. That is always an important feature of investment strategies. It is necessary to have in your library a list of typical strategies that are applicable to certain conditions. Most of these are traditional concepts observed by large and successful investment advisors, while a few are from the annals of The Legends of Wall Street (see fifth element). It is imperative that all investments be monitored continually with respect to performance. If performance changes, it is most important to adjust the investment structure accordingly. It has been postulated that **more money is lost by staying with bad investments too long than for any other reason.**

Age-Related Strategies

From the **ages of twenty to thirty**, income may be low and financial and family responsibilities high. The young investor probably has very little discretionary income left over for investing, or time to do research. At this age, there is considerable time before retirement and the investor can tolerate higher risk. Conventional wisdom recommends an above-average growth mutual fund which requires less time of the owner. To avoid the extra expense of mutual fund costs, one may consider exchange-traded closed-end funds, index funds, or Ishares, which trade like stocks. They are available for most sectors.

If there are economic downturns, young people will have sufficient time to recover. Money will be added regularly. If the fund grows at an annual rate of 10 percent for an extended period of time, it will double every seven years. For every $1 invested at age twenty-three, there will be $64 at age sixty-five. Or, to put it another way, for every $1 put in at age twenty-three, by the age of sixty there will be almost $2 worth of interest (at 6 percent) paid each year without touching the principal. The same dollar saved at age fifty-one will only be worth $4 (instead of $64). This is the magic of compounding.

Between the **ages of thirty and forty**, the paycheck improves but other expenses (mortgage, children, etc.) increase. Nevertheless, more money and time can be made available for investing. The yearly investments in growth funds may be maintained at the same level, with additional money devoted to various funds or stocks, depending on the level of investment expertise of the owner(s). More time and effort can be spent on learning about investing. The earlier the educational experience begins, the better the understanding of risk will be. A very good base of investment knowledge can be obtained.

Between the **ages of forty and fifty**, parents may find themselves funding college educations for their children, which is very expensive. Many strategies include the proposition of the children working their way through college. But for others, the savings rate will be adjusted. These are usually very good income-producing years. With ten to twenty years of accumulated investing knowledge, the investor would be expected to have a pretty good working knowledge of fundamental analysis, technical analysis, and other factors and quality of information. By the age of fifty, investors will be able to evaluate with reasonable accuracy which information is good and which is worthless. Situation- and conceptual-related strategies listed below will appeal to those interested in active investing.

From the **age fifty to retirement** are usually the best-income producing years. In addition to "socking it away" for retirement, a prudent investor will be adding a disproportionate amount of funds into more conservative investments like bonds and value stocks. An accurate assessment of lifestyle and its financial requirements is mandatory. A substantial number of investors successfully retire as early as possible when the financial production of their portfolio exceeds their requirements.

However, a significant proportion of investors find it difficult to retire because they enjoy their job, have mastered it, and are realizing substantial financial benefits. Often the surviving spouse spends the retirement savings alone.

On the other hand, if a person has accumulated forty or more years of successful investing experience, he or she can retire early and use investing experience as a "part time job" to make a few bucks on the side. There is a considerable satisfaction in trading with a small part of one's portfolio to keep one's hand still hot. Actually it's a lot easier than golf.

Situation-Related Strategies

Depressions, recessions and other financial holocausts are considered times of high risk with minimal rewards. Unemployment is high and an imbalance in the economic systems causes dislocated market forces. Even in these times there are well-managed companies who grow and are good investments. However, the majority of enterprises survive only with difficulty. Two recent such events were the Great Depression of the 1930s and the milder depression of the 1970s. Both exceeded ten years, with 1970s exhibiting four back-to-back recessions. In both cases, the investments that provided the best return were low-risk (investment grade) bonds or bond funds, CDs, insured short-term investments, savings accounts, or cash and cash equivalents.

Usually just before the beginning of a depression (during the boom times), interest rates are low. At some point an imbalance in the monetary structure takes place, which results in a shrinkage in the economy. In the 1970s, it was the oil embargo and increases in the price of oil from $2 to $30 a barrel. Political decisions often exacerbate the problem beyond the control of the Federal Reserve.

If the Federal Reserve can control the supply of money, rates will not go too much astray. But on occasion governments want to mitigate the effect of the economic shrinkage and artificially pump up the money supply. This often results in inflation. Usually stocks in building and home repair, or those that provide staples to the population, do better than others. The basic strategy is to preserve capital during this period, usually with debt instruments.

When Interest rates increase, the value of older bonds will decrease. However, when the interest rates are the highest, near the end of the recession, long-term bonds make a great investment. Many astute investors purchased thirty-year government bonds at 12 percent in 1978 and are still holding them.

During adverse economic conditions, **the absolute most important feature of any company is the quality of management.** High quality of management is the lowest risk and is explained more in the seventh element.

Periods of **booms and expansions** are the times of great wealth building. They are characterized by low interest rates, low unemployment, and high growth activities. Usually not recognized until well into the phenomena, these are also times of high productivity. Such booms occurred in the 1990s, 1950–68, 1920s, and the 1880s. The 1990s boom seemed to be due to several factors: the reallocation of capital at the end of the Cold War with Russia, the much lower oil prices after the Gulf War, and an increase in productivity of computer applications. The 1950–68 boom was probably due to reapplication of manufacturing capacity and release of pent up demand from World War 2. The 1920s boom was probably due to the beginning of large scale application of credit to build and buy houses and cars, and the 1880s boom was due to building of the railroads.

Growth stocks provided the best return on investment during these periods. Annual appreciations of 20 to 50 percent were not uncommon. Many actually believed the economic cycle had been repealed. But the exuberant generation and application of capital did produce an expansion felt all over the world. In ancient times, only the governing hierarchy usually realized the benefits of such booms. With the preponderance of the free market system, the benefits are realized by almost every one it touches. It is difficult and less important to seek good management because the high return on investment is realized more by opportunity than quality management. However, poor management will eventually find the disaster it seeks, and caution by the investor needs to be exercised so that funds are invested in actual growth-producing organizations rather than in the hype.

The **normal period** is recognized by a growth rate roughly equal to a low multiple of the population expansion, and is found between the booms and busts. During this period, it is very important to be able to recognize good management. High-quality management will provide a much better return on investment during normal times. The transition between normal periods, booms, and busts are not divided by clear demarcations. Seldom is the change from one to the other detected until a few years have passed. Also, these periods do not arrive at all parts of the country at the same time.

Conceptual-Related Strategies

Asset Allocation—This is one of the most often-quoted investment concepts. Anybody who has two different investments (like two different stocks) is allocating assets. But there is a formalized method to blend stocks, which grow faster and have more risk, with bonds, which grow slower but have lower risk. Studies have shown that such a mix will produce a return on investment only slightly lower than stocks alone in boom times but much higher than stocks in bust times. I have no data on normal times, but it would seem to be at least comparable to the average of boom and bust. This technique is dedicated to mitigating risk. As with all investments, the selection of stocks during bust times would be of prime importance. However, the asset allocation strategy appears to be a good safe investment for passive investors. The return on investment would be better than either a comparable stock or bond fund. There are funds that specialize in asset allocation.

Momentum Investing or Market Timing—This strategy is intended for those interested in using technical analysis to its fullest extent. It is effective in short-term trading and of little use in predicting long-term results. Essentially the decision-making process measures investor sentiment at a very specific time. A careful analysis of this sentiment reveals the recent emotional decisions of the investor. Many times it provides a cogent measure of the most popular fads. The astute investor's use of this information can be very profitable, but is not for the faint of heart or those who cannot exercise total discipline. Return on investment for the undisciplined can easily be negative, or poor at the least. Much like chess, luck is not involved. Smart people take money away from dumb people. More on this subject is presented in the ninth element, technical analysis.

Dollar Cost Averaging—This technique, popular many years ago, proved to be particularly fruitful for small investors. The concept is to put a fixed amount of money each month into a stock for a long period of time. Each month the number of shares purchased will vary (including fractions) depending on price fluctuations. The advantage to this strategy is that if the stock drops for any period of time, the investor buys more stock for the same amount of money, while buying less when the price is high. Over a period of several years, the investor realized a significant cost advantage. The return on investment is very good during normal or slightly slow periods. It does not work as well as other investments during bust or boom times. The problem is that an investor has to commit to a single stock for a long time and there is poor protection against deteriorating management in that stock. However, this major problem is eliminated when the philosophy is applied to funds. It is an excellent practice for developing discipline.

Penny or Low Price Stocks—Purchases generally result in a poor return on investment. People who are attracted to this type of investment also believe all people have the same capabilities and all companies perform equally. Low price is equated to a bargain and a one-cent stock going to ten cents is a 1000 percent return on investment. These stocks are marketed much like tourist traps where value is an unknown concept and sellers practice the "pump and dump" philosophy. P.T. Barnum accurately portrayed this type of investors. Passbook savings accounts at a national bank will provide a higher return on investment over the long run.

Buy and Hold—This is the old-time type of investing. The idea was to buy good stocks in good industries and hold till something went bad. My father used it for fifty-six years with considerable success. He began during the Great Depression, and died just before the boom of the 1990s. We should all be so lucky. Blue chips were the highest priced chips at the poker table, and so were named the highest priced (best) stocks on the market. Because of the high quality of management and the propensity to make a profit, blue chips were more stable and not as prone to investing fads and fancies. The lower volatility attracts mostly long-term stable investors, and few traders and speculators.

The first step was to determine good industries. This is a simple rational observation of the country's economy. During the period from 1900 to 1930 the country expanded greatly, and companies producing goods that supported these activities prospered greatly. These included railroads, steel, oil, and later, automobiles. The object was to buy stocks in the largest companies in these fields, because they had the most control of their future.

Big companies get big because they do something well, and people will pay for that. The anathema against big companies their attempt to guarantee mediocrity. Growth is a sign of efficient use of available resources. Most investment decisions using this strategy are based on fundamental analysis. Many investment clubs and similar organizations use this strategy.

The problem with the Buy and Hold philosophy is twofold. First, it is difficult to recognize when the industry performance is well past its prime and is contracting. An example is the steel industry, which was in ascendancy when the country needed rails, cars, and steel war materials in the early twentieth century. When steel became a commodity and more value was in electronics, plastics, aluminum, other items, the popular belief was that the decline was not caused by less use, but by unfair competition.

The second problem is that a well-managed company in that industry may appear to be more productive than it really is because the change is so gradual. Also, if a company's management is dedicated to survival, it can mask reduced performances for a long period of time by blaming others, or manipulating the books. The Buy and Hold strategy does not easily lend itself to the upgrading of a portfolio and purging of deteriorating companies. The lag time between performance and action causes investors to stay with a faulty investment too long.

Value Investing—Made popular by Warren Buffet, Value Investing is an improved version of the Buy and Hold philosophy. He seeks undervalued stocks using fundamental analysis (eighth element), with the intention of holding for a lifetime. There are literally tons of books on the subject (one written by Janet Lowe is mentioned later). Value Investing also considers the function of the company in the economy and aims specifically where value is gauged by the consistent ability to produce profits.

Buffet has often opined that he does not buy companies he doesn't understand. In this way he is able to determine if the words of some financial advisor are accurate or just a bunch of fluff. Also, he includes "franchise value" as part of the overall value of the investment. Franchise value is the amount extra a customer will pay to guarantee product satisfaction.

Typical examples include Coca Cola, Gillette, MacDonald's, WalMart, and IBM.

One offshoot of this philosophy considers the situation in which the price reaches a calculated "value," the stock is sold, and the funds recycled to other undervalued companies. The "growth" of these companies is mostly realized when they go from undervalued to overvalued. However, Buffet expresses the intention to hold a company forever (but not without checking closely and often).

This strategy solves the problem with the Buy and Hold strategy, and has proved to be relatively easy to use and low risk. For less experienced investors, the emphasis on understanding the business enhances the learning process. In addition, if the selling of overvalued companies is enforced, it provides a rational discipline profitable for all investors. It is a highly recommended strategy for all investors, and has proven to be eminently successful.

The problem (if it could be considered one) is that it misses opportunities in advanced technologies or concepts, which are difficult to understand. Many new enterprises of higher risk and high potential reward will automatically be excluded because of the inability to calculate traditional value. But many astute investors compensate by investing the majority of their portfolios using the value criteria and assign a small portion of their funds to the entrepreneurial spirit.

Gardening—Don Worden assigned the term "gardening" to the process I used in the correspondence to the TC 2000 forum during July 2000. The name refers to the pruning process used to replace stocks. It is a minor adjustment to the Buy-Hold and Value strategies. The idea was to reduce the amount of work for an individual investor and improve the quality of investment success, while allowing expansion into areas Buffet would not tread.

It is nothing new, but is based on the idea that a lot of information about a few things is more profitable than a little information about a lot of things. The purpose is to minimize risk and maximize returns by using all eleven elements of prudent investing. It is applicable to several strategies, and it is directed to the active investor with limited time and resources.

The first step is to select a universe of about thirty to seventy stocks, funds, and indexes. Try to make a representation of the market in general with a bias toward blue chip stocks. This universe will be reviewed daily or weekly. It must be small enough for the investor familiar with this universe to perform the review in a short period of time (fifteen minutes to half an hour a day), yet large enough to appraise the market forces. A typical example would include:

1. Four to ten market indexes like the Dow-30, S&P 500, Nasdaq, Dow Bond index, five-year notes, Commodity Bureau Index, and the U.S. Dollar Index.

2. Perhaps three to ten funds (closed or open ended) specializing in sectors like technology, gold, utilities, and foreign countries like Germany, Japan, and Mexico. There is a dual purpose to selecting these funds. First is to determine which sectors are doing well, and second, they provide a source for favored stocks (by discovering the fund's largest holdings).

3. The remaining thirty to sixty selections will be a variety of large and small companies. Usually we start with the blue chips from the Dow Jones Industrials or another source of well-managed companies. A wise selection would include some of the largest (900-pound Gorillas) from a list of sectors which may include technology, transportation, manufacturing, health, insurance, financial, retail, telecommunications, utilities, and energy. The majority should be large-cap successful companies, with a smattering of smaller enterprises and midcaps stocks. This will allow comparisons between different industries, between companies within an industry, and between larger and smaller companies.

The next step is to perform a thorough fundamental analysis on each item to determine the comparative value within and between groups. I look at this as a farmer preparing the soil for planting crops. A good effort early will insure better productivity later. It is important to know these stocks as if they were members of your family. Between the internet and the library, there is a plethora of information available to anyone who wants to learn (more than you would ever want to know).

This initial investigation should not be hurried, but thoughtful and meticulous. The more comprehensive the investigation, the more it will become obvious that certain of these stocks (or funds) have a better value to price relationship, with lower risk. The half-dozen best stocks become the portfolio, and their entry point can be determined by technical analysis. This thorough analysis does not have to be repeated very often, just periodically updated, a process which takes much less time. These updates are just looking for differences.

Each day or week, depending on the investor, a quick look at the technical charts of each item in the universe should be taken, with special attention given to those in the portfolio. If it is done often, the investor will become very familiar with the personality and trend of each stock/index and it will be relatively easy to recognize if there is a potential deviation from the initial investigation, or a change in stock/index's character. The relationship between your portfolio and each index will become natural. Any change will become a red flag and prompt an update to the information base.

Perhaps the greatest benefit comes when listening to a commentator on TV or while reading a publication when one of the items from your universe is discussed. It is like hearing your name mentioned in a crowd. The additional information will add to your base of information. It may confirm what you already know, or provide you with new information. If you are thoroughly knowledgeable of the company's activities, you will be better able to evaluate the information. You will know where to go to corroborate the information. If false, you can discard it.

Since technical analysis measures investor sentiment, many times a potential problem is forecast by a change in the charts. A drastic move in either direction is usually matched by a news announcement at a later time. If you are forewarned, you can pursue the problem and be among the first to know. If there is an unexpected change, a prudent investor will update all the factors from the fundamental analysis. An additional investigation of the stock, the competitor's stock, or the industry will usually indicate the cause of the reaction. If determined to be adverse, then the stock can be "pruned" and replaced with a stronger performer.

On occasion, it will be noted that there is not a change in fundamentals, and the rapid negative change in the price action was the result of traders responding to an artificial influence "to make something happen." Investors without this knowledge may panic and sell when it was not called for. Other more knowledgeable investors may see this as an opportunity to add to a position at the expense of the traders exiting a short position.

Armed with this knowledge, a prudent investor will be able to make a better call as to whether to vacate the position or to hold through the event. It minimizes costly panic reactions. However, when panic is called for, the investor will know the reason. More discussion on this phenomena will be covered under the fourth element, Quality of Information.

When an adverse discovery is made, the most important question is: "If I knew this before, would I have bought the stock?" or "Would I buy the stock now?". If the answer is no, then it's time to sell. The new price is a better gauge of true value.

The gardening procedure takes place during these technical and fundamental reviews. When a portfolio is strong, it is not necessary to do this analysis every day. However, it is so easy to let it slide, and before too long, all the information is outdated and the quality of decisions suffers. Small doses of study are much less painless than a concentrated effort.

The performance of all investments will change over time. Many can be held for years through up and down cycles. Often it will become apparent that it is better to weather a downdraft rather than sell and pay the income taxes due. But all stocks are candidates for replacement. (Falling in love with an investment is usually an expensive luxury). When the decision is made to prune a stock from the portfolio, another is planted. A portfolio is being constantly reviewed for upgrade.

Stocks that are discarded from the portfolio are always potential candidates for future inclusion. Sometimes a very good stock has had a very good run of several years and the CEO retires, or gets sick and leaves. It usually takes a year or two for the culture to adapt to a new CEO. During this period the stock needs to "rest" for a while.

Also there may be a shift in the macroeconomic conditions, like an energy crisis. One would expect the portfolio to change in order to adapt to the new conditions. This applies not just in oil and gas stocks, but in utilities, automobile manufacturers, and possibly defense industries. Later, when the crisis or war is over, the character of the universe will change again.

The key to all strategies is to pay attention and practice discipline.

Tax Strategies

Generally, tax strategies consist of buying tax-free bonds,—sheltered investments, IRA's, 401Ks, etc. All are well known and several good books are available on the subject. Most investors do quite well in these areas. However, one area prone to failure is the avoidance of taking a loss. Except for some very unusual circumstances, it is the best strategy to take all the losses prior to the end of the year.

A lot of people buy a stock and it goes down. They may hold it for years hoping it will go back up. They hate to admit they have made a mistake. There are different ways of handling this problem. If you have good reason to believe the stock will go back up faster than other investments, then keep it. The first question to ask is: if you had not owned the stock, you would buy it now? If the answer no, then selling is usually the best option.

If you feel that the stock is a good investment, you may buy more at the lower price. If you want to hold your position and not put in more money, but take advantage of the stock loss, you can do that by a simple procedure. Thirty days before the end of the year, buy an equal amount of the same stock. Wait those thirty days and sell the first batch. Now you have the stock at the lower basis and still have the deduction for a tax loss. The thirty-day wait is necessary to avoid the "wash" rule.

Strategy Conclusions

The strategy most likely to succeed is a combination of one or more of those shown above, and perhaps some not shown. It should be tailored to the investor's needs, wants, and abilities. Most of the rudiments described under "Gardening" can be useful with all the strategies. In addition to selecting the best strategy, it is also necessary to execute it properly. To do this takes discipline.

The worst offence is to buy something, watch it go down, and plan to wait till it comes back up to sell. It went down because its value has diminished. The market has already determined that. When a stock (or any investment) has made an adverse change in character it must be sold as soon as possible. Granted you may wait a bit for a bounce, but the decision has been made to sell, and all we're waiting for is the execution.

This rule applies to long-term investors as well as traders. Having money tied up for extended periods of time destroys the return on investment equation. Typically one-third of the investment decisions will probably be wrong, through no fault of the investor. If an investor gets out of the bad ones as soon as possible and lets the good ones ride, he or she can do extremely well.

I usually avoid presenting personal examples but many years ago (I think during the 1970s), I made several bad trading decisions in a row, so I decided to take a rest. I took most of my money and put it into a stogy chemical company named DOW. I had planned to sit and rest a few months until I could get my house in order. I had started to do paper trading. Scarcely three days later, they announced a massive isocyanate leak at a Dow Chemical plant in India, which killed over one thousand people.

The stock was halted and opened the next day at fifteen, down from forty-eight the day before. C'est la vie.

Any successful strategy will include:

1. A reasonable look at your own common sense and discipline,
2. Your ability to assign the responsibility to someone else or to yourself,
3. The consideration of your age,
4. A reasonable look at your risk tolerance,
5. A selection of an investment strategy (value etc), and
6. A realistic look at whether you should be a passive or active investor.

All strategies have strong and weak points. Much like selecting a friend, pick the weak points or faults you can live with. **The most common failure is the lack of an exit procedure, where an investor intends to keep a stock that has depreciated until the loss is recovered. An exit procedure is essential to successful investing.** The earlier this exit decision is made, the lower the negative effect will be on the portfolio.

Technical analysis can be of great use to a long-term fundamental or Value investor because it can provide early warning to adverse circumstances. Usually the change in fundamental character is predicted by the charts, which are then followed by the actual changes. These changes may be good or bad. Sometimes these changes are the fault of management. Other times it is due to macroeconomic events or market forces. However, there are occasions where the investor just made a bad decision by not doing his homework properly. That has happened to everybody. The required action is the same for all three circumstances: get out!

FOURTH ELEMENT—QUALITY OF INFORMATION

Truth is the single most important element in Human development

The Problem

Have you ever read or heard on TV a positive review of a company that indicated it to be a good buy? After thoughtful consideration and more investigation, you purchased the stock. Not too long after, it drifted down, but the media kept encouragement high with additional recommendations. Perhaps six months later, the stock dropped 40 percent, and a few articles appeared to indicate some problems, but the large majority of analysts still recommended the stock. Five more months go by and the stock is now down 70 percent, but some analysts are still recommending the stock.

Granted this is an unusual event, but it recently happened to several Internet-related stocks during the period from the spring of 2000 to the spring of 2001. Mary Meeker and Henry Blodget, two highly rated analysts specializing in Internet stocks working for major investment houses, did make the kind of recommendations described above. It has been reported on the news that one side of the investment house was providing services to these companies with the intent of increasing the value of the stock, while the other side was performing what was reputed to be independent analysis for stockholders. In addition, it appears the salaries of these analysts were related to their recommendations.

The legal adventures involving these two resulted in Henry's brokerage settling out of court, and Mary's case being thrown out. Insufficient evidence was the reported cause, but the investor's understanding of his responsibilities and due diligence (discussed later) is an absolute necessity for successful investing.

Background

In order to better appreciate the problem of assessing quality of information with respect to investing, we need to understand a little more about the industry involved. These people who affect the decision-makers in companies all over the world are the same as those around you. They have about the same distribution of saints and sinners, competents and incompetents, conservatives and liberals as the rest of the world. True, some management cultures tend to skew those ratios a little toward one side or another, but this business is composed of all kinds of folks.

In the past, it was the practice for companies to give advanced information to the more important analysts for use in their recommendations. This was done to avoid law suits, which may be incurred because of forward-looking statements. A forward-looking statement would be something akin to a prediction indicating that in next quarter, the earnings may be pretty good (or bad). The more successful analysts were followed carefully by other analysts, resulting in a herd mentality. The belief seemed to be that it has to be true because THEY said it.

Here is a typical example of a procedure practiced many years ago. A company officer is responsible for creating an accurate image of his company. If he predicts potential future events which do not take place, even if there was a high probability of occurrence when the prediction was made, he may be held financially liable. If the company officer gave the analysts this kind of advanced information, the analyst can create a positive (or negative) impression about the future without the same potential liabilities. If the information is positive, the analyst would say something like,

"This stock is VERY interesting". The code words would mean go out and mortgage your wife and children and buy this stock. Later, the company would make a public announcement as to the actual numbers. If the analyst was right, he appeared as a hero, someone "in the know."

If the news was bad or just neutral, the analyst could put a little spin on it to make it look not quite that bad. The more astute investors would have better information and sell, while the average small-time investor would receive the news gracefully and often wonder why the stock was falling on news that did not really seem that bad. It may take a year or more before the problem is solved, meanwhile the price languished and the return on investment was poor for those seeking their own information.

Each brokerage house would have its analyst who gave recommendations to the brokers, and most investors would get the information from the brokers. However, it was noted that very large investors would do better and get their information a little ahead of the smaller investors. Technical analysis would allow traders to see this unusual activity in the action of a stock, and reasonable predictions of what was about to happen could be made before the announcement. The adage of "Buy on the rumor and sell on the news" is the result of traders applying this kind of analysis because it would be reasonable to expect a stock to jump a little based on good news. The less affluent investor could do reasonably well by using technical analysis for short-term predictions. However, the real effective long-term strategy was still based on fundamental analysis and high-quality management.

Often, a brokerage house had accumulated a quantity of "dogs" in the brokerage account that needed to be eliminated. In the days long ago, brokers on occasions would recommend a stock that was a real dud along with some good recommendations. Many times it was a company that you'd never heard of, or a company having financial problems. The broker would recommend it "for your consideration," indicating he thought it really had promise and that the company's troubles were over. After holding it for a year or so while it lost value, you would eventually sell. It is postulated that these dogs were spread rather evenly among the less astute investors.

During this same period, the broker would recommend other lesser known stocks, which would flourish. Your portfolio would prosper or disappoint depending on whether it was a bear or bull market. It was very difficult to tell which of these recommended stocks were good or bad investments. Value Line (usually available at the public library) was a very popular (and expensive) service, which helped considerably. Good technical analysis was difficult to obtain for small investors, and usually was limited to point and figure charts. The most successful investors were the ones with good brokers or large portfolios who could afford good analysts.

In the 1990s discount brokers became popular, soon followed by Internet investing and analysis. The knowledge gap closed rapidly, but the analysts still had advanced information rights. However, the average investor could now gather good information about most companies in a relatively short period of time, and those interested could challenge the potential of an investment. Until recently, when the federal government ruled that all forward-looking information had to be revealed to everyone at the same time, the broker's information was more valuable. Even with all information becoming available to the small investor, the broker still does have an advantage. First he has superior judgment available with which to apply to the information, and he can get the appropriate information faster. It is reasonable to assume that the judgment and speed factors are applied to larger portfolios more efficiently than to smaller ones.

In addition to having better information sooner, the larger brokerage houses could also create self-fulfilling prophecies in a stock that may not be a particularly good investment. Just the force of a large number of accounts that received a recommendation in advance and invested a lot of money over a short period of time could cause a stock to move. A technical analyst would pick that move, hop on the bandwagon, and a snowball effect could be promoted. The possibility of efficiently unloading unproductive stocks still exists.

Efficient Market Theory

A word needs to be said about Efficient Market Theory. This theory says the present price reflects all information and expectations about a stock. Any kind of analysis cannot improve on it, therefore, it is impossible to do better than the averages or indexes. If this were so, then the traditional Gaussian distribution curves would not apply. If there weren't so many people (and funds) beating the averages consistently, it would be a good idea.

The failure of this concept is due to several factors, including the reality that the quantity and quality of information is not available to, nor will reach, all investors at the same time. Therefore all investors do not come to the same conclusion at the same time. Investor's beliefs are the primary forces affecting price. Also lying by analysts is an inhibiting factor.

But the concept of the market becoming consistently more efficient is correct. This is due to the improved judgments wrought from communication improvements over time. The most recent example is the Internet, where better and faster information transfers improves the ability to draw accurate conclusions, thereby infusing a higher truth-value to an analytical conclusion about a stock. Consider truth-value to be the quantitative percentage of truth in a statement. One of the forces impeding the Efficient Market Theory is the psychological factor based more on irrational exuberance than truthful analysis.

Due Diligence

How many people do you know who do not want to worry about stocks? They say, "I just want someone to manage my money." This passive attitude is common, but it does not absolve a person from their responsibility of due diligence. Due diligence means you are responsible for all mistakes made, including those where you misinterpreted what I said. For example, assume you asked me if XYZ was a buy, hold, or sell, and I answered the following: "The company is expected to earn $2 a share, we expect their revenue to be up 12 percent, and they are leaders in their market; yes, we consider it a buy with a target of $40."

Before you buy it, you need to check to see if they will earn $2 per share, have a high probability of increasing their revenue by 12 percent, and a high probability of remaining a leader of their market. If you did not analyze it and the numbers are different and you bought it and it went down, it's your fault. If you analyzed it and the numbers are the same and it went down, it's not my fault because the conclusion was rational based on those numbers. The other investors who sold are at fault for not recognizing a good investment. If my numbers are not rational, your analysis should show that and you should not have bought the stock.

Also, a target is something to shoot at, not a guarantee. In other words, you have to do your homework and draw the conclusions. All statements like the above are disqualifiers. But one thing you do know is that he has probably recommended it to others before he recommended it to you (unless you have a very sizeable portfolio). If you got the information free, rest assured that you were (are) at the bottom end of the financial food chain. Quite often, a technical analysis will reveal the stock has already moved substantially before you got this recommendation. It is entirely probable that the analyst was trying to improve a stock that he really believes is good, and he had previously recommended it to his paying customers. They seldom (if ever) tell investors when to sell.

Once an astute investor has achieved a reasonable level of proficiency in investigating stocks with due diligence in mind, it is relatively easy to determine the value of an investment and the accuracy of the recommendation. Also, please realize that a commentator who recommends a stock is speaking to a generic investor. His recommendation will probably not be applicable to all individuals. It is important for the investor to know which recommendations apply to him. A well-grounded strategy based on a thoughtful goal will allow an investor to avoid spending a lot of superfluous time and energy on non-applicable information and make the due diligence investigation less of a drag.

Many prefer the passive investing approach by getting someone else to gather and apply the technical and fundamental information. The passive investors do this by buying funds with the same investment objectives as theirs. They still have to perform due diligence on the selection and performance of the fund, but this is generally much easier. There are very reputable services like Morningstar that specialize in keeping up with the performance of nearly all publicly traded funds. All funds state their goals, objectives, strategies, and risks. These are ranked with ratings from one to five stars with five indicating the best performers. Information on the fund's holdings, history, and management personnel is available, with high truth-value in all categories. But there is a price to pay. All funds charge a fee, which is a small price for those not interested in performing due diligence. But you have the responsibility of due diligence on the fund.

Finally, if you try anything in this book and it fails, it's your fault.

Market Operations

Over at least the last hundred years, the market has had a long-term uptrend. The market normally operates with rather sedate trends pretty well in concert with the earnings of the various companies. This has been interrupted on occasions with downturns caused by macroeconomic imbalances resulting in recessions or depressions. During these interruptions there is a distinct separation between the well-performing companies and all others. Often the investors' reaction turns from irrational exuberance to panic motivated by fear and greed, the two most effective forces driving the market.

Many analysts and commentators try to avoid the negative panic by painting a picture perhaps a little more rosy than necessary. This may be a disservice. Panic (up or down) is a reaction based on lack of knowledge. It has sometimes happened that a person sees the market retreat and sells all his stocks because others are doing the same. Deprived of the lack of understanding of market reaction, these people will usually sell at the bottom. Due diligence, not only on the stocks but also with the markets, prevents this problem. Truthful knowledge (sometimes called wisdom) is the objective.

With a little effort one can determine the character of management, and make a lucid assessment of the quality of management (Seventh Element). Few people would stand for having crooks manage their money, so successful crooks appear to be honest. Dishonest management may exist for a while, but eventually they go out of business or change.

However, it is difficult to differentiate between mediocre management and good management under all conditions. It is especially difficult to discern this difference during boom times, because performance differences are often small. The good fortune of being at the right place at the right time is nearly equal to good management during this period. However, as the market conditions deteriorate, the differences become more discernable, and in bad times very obvious. Owning well-managed companies is the best immunization against adverse macroeconomic or market forces.

The Plan to Get Quality Information

When we gather information, we need to know about whom and about what. Then we need to know how truthful the information is, and how applicable it is. In the case of investing, quantity will never be a substitute for quality. Having large quantities of information, much of which may be irrelevant, is more of a problem than not having anything. When you don't have any information, you know you're in trouble. When you have a lot, you may be deceiving yourself into believing you know more than you really do. Gathering information is like playing golf or some other self-challenging sport. You never become perfect at it, but with careful and thoughtful effort, you steadily improve each time you do it. The more you do it, the better you get.

An efficient method for managing the truth gathering process is to use the management by exception philosophy. In this philosophy, a careful and complete plan is devised with stops set to evaluate progress. It is of utmost importance to spend enough time to develop a well thought out plan that includes contingencies and/or alternate considerations. Then the plan is executed and the majority of the management effort is spent determining and addressing (solving) exceptions to the original plan. Minimal time is spent on the part that is performing in accordance with the originally plan. All good plans are relatively simple.

Such a plan may begin with establishing evaluation criteria based on the goals of the strategy. Using return on investment (ROI) as a major (but not total) criteria, we assess the potential value of a specific company on its ability to produce a return comparable to the industry norm.

Consider the investigation of investments in alternate energy like windmills or solar power. It would be tempting to put a high value on a company in this area as a potential "Microsoft" which will grow with extreme fervor. It is relatively easy to discover several utility companies buying windmills to develop energy farms. With a little effort, and disregarding the hype of "good for the country" etc., we discover the ROI of windmills is about 20 percent less than oil, 40 percent less than coal, and much less than nuclear. The nuclear is undetermined because of safety concerns.

Without much work, it is easy to discover that solar power is from seven to ten times more expensive than conventional power generation. Additional research reveals the oil /gas reserves have increased substantially since the first oil crisis of the 1970s, and there is not really an energy shortage, but a distribution/price crisis. Although environmental catastrophes are not imminent, the problem is out there. Finally, a considerable amount of work has improved the ROI for alternate energy sources as well as pollution abatement of coal usage. Soon we find that the problem is not one of investment or performance, but the politics involved with the relationship between energy and the environment.

The investor cannot solve this (political) problem, and a prudent investor will stand aside until the political problems are resolved or at least manageable. He may not make as much, but also will not lose by being on the wrong side. This is a risk reduction decision. It is not necessary to appraise all sides of the political arguments. It does not take much time or resources to determine this is not a prudent investment at this time. But the information and evaluation criteria is there for future situations, when the time arrives.

Spending a few hours over a few days developed the above information. Much more information was reviewed, but all that did not apply to the ultimate criteria (ROI) was not considered. No time was spent on the efficacy of the respective arguments. The value of these arguments does not effect the sought-after conclusion, that is, whether an investor should commit funds to this enterprise.

When investigating a stock, look to see how the information fits, and what conclusions the information supports. Look for exceptions rather than confirming data. Look for the preponderance of evidence to throw out the stock. Divergences are the most important attributes to assess the truth. Eventually all divergences will get resolved. The unresolved divergences are the source and measure of the risk. They must be resolved or evaluated in order to make a cogent investment. The successful technique is to determine the resolution before it's too late. With such a wide variety of investments available, **often it is more prudent to walk away from an irreconcilable difference than to guess the outcome.** There is always another day.

Because we are dealing with human foibles, we need to consider the laws of probabilities. Expecting a high level of certitude is unreasonable. The doubt may apply to oneself. "What if I'm wrong?" needs to be an element of the investment procedure and strategy. Fear of being wrong is not a reason to avoid investing. Consider two potential investments, one in which you would make a lot of money if you succeed, and lose a smaller amount if you fail. The second investment would make a lesser amount (than the first) if you succeed and would make a very small amount of you fail. The prudent investor would choose the second and the riverboat gambler would choose the first. You can construct your investments to mitigate risk.

A healthy dose of skepticism is an essential element of any analysis, and is more important in the stock market arena. The reason is that most of our decisions are made based on what other people are doing or thinking. All stocks go up or down based primarily on the buy or sell decisions a lot of people make at that time. Greed, fear, fads, fickle notions, and any other irrational feelings affect these people. It is reasonable to approach every significant item with a feeling of doubt, regardless of source. As stated above, truth is the single most important element in human development. It is no more important anywhere else than it is in investing. When doubt is removed, one no longer seeks the truth.

FIFTH ELEMENT—LEGENDS OF WALL STREET

A legend is defined as a story coming down from the past, a popular myth, or a person or thing that inspires legends. However, it is also a list of explanatory symbols on a map intended to assist the traveler in a more pleasant and safe journey. The following list qualifies as all of the above.

Generally legends are handed down from generation to generation, and are presented as cautionary warnings dedicated to minimizing risk. A couple examples include: "Never trust a skinny cook" and "Red sky in the morning, sailors take warning, red sky at night, sailors delight."

However, this is a list of legends applies to investing. I heard the first part of them from my mother and father. They are presented pretty much in the order in which I learned them. Later I accumulated others and have found them to be useful. I've found violating these precepts is woefully expensive. I would give credit to the originators, if I knew or could remember who they were.

1. Pity the man who wins the first time at a horse race (he thinks he knows how to win).
2. Do not buy controversial companies (never be stampeded into buying a company; take time to research it. If a company is in the news for any problem, avoid it).
3. Buy Quality ("A" stocks as shown in the Standard and Poor stock guide).
4. Never fall in love with a company (be objective and always willing to sell).
5. If you don't profit from your mistakes, someone else will.

6. Dogs run before the crash (Companies with no earnings and poor prospects go up in price just before the market makes a large correction or crash. Corrections and crashes correct the problem of overpriced stocks.)
7. Good today, good tomorrow (You can wait to buy a good company. Good companies stay good companies for a long time. You never have to hurry up to buy).
8. Bulls make money, bears make money, and pigs get slaughtered.
9. Buy in December and sell in May.
10. Avoid buying during the months of September and October.
11. Buy good companies in good industries.
12. Growth rate should equal Price-to-Earnings ratio. (PE ratio of twenty should equal a 20 percent earnings growth rate; this can be adjusted for interest rates).
13. Don't buy stocks on emotions; instead use knowledge to avoid irrational exuberance.
14. Don't fight the tape (when the market is going down, don't try to guess the turning point before it's actually turned).
15. Hold, don't trade or time investments.
16. As January goes, so goes the rest of the year.
17. As September goes, be contrary.
18. First hour amateurs, last hour professionals (this is during the day).
19. When a stock breaks (falls), wait three days for the rebound.
20. Never catch a falling knife. (See 6, 19)
21. Look for the double bottom (or top). It is a sign the trend has changed.
22. Buy stocks two years before the election and treasuries the following two years.
23. Only the paranoid survive. (Andy Grove of Intel)

And last the legend most everyone has heard before: If it seems too good to be true, it probably is.

SIXTH ELEMENT—GURUS

Originally this element was to have been part of the Fourth Element: Quality of Information, but because of its unique effect on investing it has been classified as a separate element. The information from Gurus is neither good nor bad, but must be considered in context after a strategy has been decided upon.

This is a element seldom recognized by most investors, but can be of great value if used properly. Guru is a term used to describe one of those analytical experts who publish in the papers, on TV and /or on the Internet about investments and issue buy or sell recommendations on specific stocks. This does not include those experts who are selling their books on investing or are experts who teach a cautious or prudent philosophy of investing. Subscribed investors or an investment house usually pays for the Guru's advice, but often it's free on a delayed basis to the general public. They usually make a rational case for a specific stock, the economy, an industry, or some other investment like gold or bonds.

Experience has shown that to buy or sell based on a guru's advice is no better than flipping a coin, even though some may have a run of luck for awhile. Of course they would like to succeed and thereby bring in more customers. But there is another conclusion easily drawn. Perhaps they give their advice first to paying customers, and then give it out for free later to increase demand for the stock. They very seldom accurately pick out tops and bottoms. However, their advice is not always wrong, either. Usually expectations exceed performance.

The really bad lesson learned from taking this kind of advice is that the Guru is not there to tell you when to sell. On more than one occasion I have bought a stock and rode it up and down, not knowing that I should have sold before it was too late. I suspect the Guru told his subscribers when to sell. Generally, a careful periodic review of the stock on a fundamental and/or technical basis would have indicated that it is not a buy and hold, and was good only for trading. Gurus normally do not recommend the buy and hold portfolios. Most Gurus never recommend top blue chips like Coca Cola, Proctor and Gamble, General Electric, or Merck. When these stocks are going up, they say their PE is too high and to wait until the price pulls back. When the stock languishes for awhile, they always say to wait till it recovers.

The most valuable piece of information to learn about the Guru is that you can safely conclude he has recommended it to his paying clients before he gave it to you. However, there has been more than one occasion on which I suspected the stock was recommended because an important client had a bunch to sell and the Guru was helping to get rid of it. Cynicism and paranoia are important to successful investing.

It is highly recommended for the investor to learn how to make a buy decision on his own so he can make a valid determination on when to sell. If you don't know why you bought it, you don't know why you should sell it.

Having said all of the above, I have had some success when using the paid services of a Guru. The key feature is that the Guru was giving sell signals also. If he does provide sell signals, it may well be a credible service worth using. There is another advantage in this type of service: it consists of self-fulfilling prophecies. If the Guru has a large following, he will actually generate movement in the stock simply by issuing the buy or sell order.

Henry Blodget and Mary Meeker were such Gurus. Particularly during the heyday of the Internet craze, this procedure was popular and successful. Check out if the company is making money. Even two years after the dot-com bubble burst, some of these advisory services were still issuing strong buys on stocks (Yahoo) that had revenue drops of 35+ percent, no earnings, poor prospects, and price to sales of fourteen. Within seven days the stock rose 42 percent. Remember due diligence.

Seventh Element—The Quality of Company Management

The most important asset of a company is the management

Making an assessment of the quality of company management is a most important task. It's difficult because of the subjective nature of the undertaking. Since the management is made up of people rather than numbers, it is necessary to form opinions of what people will do under varied, sometimes untried circumstances. In assessment of macroeconomics and market forces, we look at the average performances of large numbers of people, which is easier than learning the quality of the few top managers. However, in determining the quality of management, it is necessary to know the leadership.

The first important factor is to determine their ability to use resources most efficiently. If your company uses resources more efficiently than a competitor while the sales price is the same, your company will produce more profit. Or to put it another way, he will be the low cost producer. However, comparing costs is a nightmare and gets into the problem of trying to compare the results of widely differing cost structures. It is necessary to establish a comparison based on a common value, that is money.

The resources a company has to work with are; money, labor (which is satisfied with money), and materials (which is acquired with money). Therefore, the most often used attribute to assess management is the effective use of money, or return on investment. The higher return on investment, the more efficiently the money is being used.

For the investor this is a calculated number in fundamental analysis (Eighth Element) and may be referred to as total return, which includes dividends. It is prudent to consider this number for several periods of time, such as one, three, and five years, to determine management consistency. By comparing the ROI of a company to other companies, industries, and the general market, it becomes easier to compare management of different companies with some standard.

Consider company management to be a fundamental attribute, much like PE ratios, or earning growth rates. **When you buy a stock, you are not buying a software system, a bunch of oil wells, a gold mine, a group of buildings, or anything material. You are buying the ability of the top management in the company to acquire and run all of the above-mentioned businesses while producing a reasonable profit at an acceptable risk.**

Good management will discover an acceptable number of oil wells, etc. and provide an acceptable return on the equity for the shareholders. Lesser or average management will not have the ability to put these assets to work as efficiently or may even squander the opportunities. Bad management will usually cheat you out of your money.

Good is a subjective term. Just to get listed on an exchange and conduct business, a company has to be pretty good. Almost all listed companies are good in that they produce profits and grow at some level. Most companies have a lot of good and loyal people. But we are not only interested in avoiding good companies that have fallen into bad hands (read Enron), we are also interested in investing in only those companies that consistently perform above average through different market conditions, and that continue to perform well in bad market conditions.

This type of management is the result of an intended effort to develop a culture of superior leadership. One characteristic of all organizations (good or bad), is that culture tends to take on the character of its chief executive. Therefore, good management tends to beget good management, just as poor management also tends to propagate itself. The quality of the management is developed primarily by the demand of the stockholders through the board of directors.

One of the situations that illustrate good quality management is to observe how it reacts to an adverse condition. A positive response and rapid adaptability to an emergency situation is an encouraging sign of a desired quality culture. Reflect on how JNJ addressed the Tylenol scare several years ago. Within six months it was all over. Their first order of business was to protect the customer by having all Tylenol on the store shelves sent back to the company, even though there was no evidence of a manufacturing problem. They met the problem head on, solved it, and got back to the business of selling drugs.

On the other hand, stonewalling, delayed response, and foot dragging are signs of poor quality of culture. Again reflect on the Ford/Firestone tire problem on the Explorers. Hundreds of lives were lost and irreparable damage was done to both companies. Both Ford and Firestone exhibited poor management by trying to shun responsibility rather than protect the customer. Loyal customers are the second most important asset of any company.

If the auto companies were well managed, the Japanese auto companies could not have come to North America in the early 1970s and take away 30 percent of the auto business. The arrogance of the auto companies during the oil crisis of the 1970s cost them a large portion of the business. Well-managed companies realize the customers are driving the boat, while arrogant companies believe they are.

Management has the goal and responsibility to produce profits; good management does it for the long run, mostly by building brand loyalty, and the rest of the companies operate with a much shorter viewpoint.

An article in the 1997 March/April issue of *Harvard Business Review* by Arie de Geus, a retired group planning coordinator for Royal Dutch Shell Group (RD), titled "The Living Company," reports on the characteristics of corporations that will live a long time. These include but are not limited to:

1. The development of a management culture that can change easily to meet changing conditions,
2. The development of low-risk ventures (The more the preparation the lower the risk),
3. Sensitivity to the world around them, and awareness of its identity (don't get too big for your britches),
4. Tolerance of new ideas (avoid the "not invented here" syndrome),
5. Loose steering and control (let the young guys try a few things. Even if they do fail, it's a cheap education), and
6. Organization for learning, and shaping the human community of the company.

This last characteristic means that the company develops the employees through education and varied experiences and allows them to improve themselves.

RD, which was a spin-off of the old East India Company of the 1600s, took the present form over one hundred years ago and grew to be the largest (Market Cap) company in the world by the early 1990s. They traditionally look as much as fifty years in advance, considering such things as what business they will be in when oil runs out. RD will be there because they plan to be there.

The credo at the Bendix Corp in their 1975 annual report was that people were their most important asset. To most, Bendix was considered a "people company," where a person's word was of great value. **In all good companies integrity is all-important because they depend on a person fulfilling their word.** In a well-managed company you never see the procedure having to put something in writing to make sure it gets done. Lack of integrity is dealt with swiftly.

Good management will not have an adversarial relationship with its employees, while poor management squeezes everything possible out of them. There is no room for voluntary product improvements under poor management. In the first half of the twentieth century, steel companies were among the biggest and strongest and most aggressive. Because of poor management, we now import a large amount of steel, and most of U.S. steel companies are either in bankruptcy, part of another company, or inconsequential. Bad management causes unions. Well-managed companies may have unions, but seldom have union problems.

Well-managed companies avoid controversy and stick to their knitting, i.e. increasing shareholder value. That is their reason for existence. Politics mixed with business generally produces poor return on investment and often generates unwanted enemies. Often, social engineering activists attack large companies to blackmail them into political positions. A well-managed company will avoid this trap because it is a lose-lose proposition.

These activists want the company to make it company policy to never make nuclear bomb parts, or to hire a fixed number of minorities, or to stop using coal, etc. The belief is that if the largest company does sets the example, then others will follow. A perusal of the proponents of such propositions reveals a dearth of business knowledge. Rather than follow the leader, competitors would view this as a weakness and seize the opportunity to knock off the big boy on the block. Succumbing to such propositions indicates weak management and predicts failure.

Finally, many people think of successful companies as having unprincipled, aggressive, and unscrupulous management. This is patently not true. There are some companies that are led by such people and have reaped large rewards for short periods of time. There are countries led by rulers with the same qualities and same results. But in the long run, the truly well-managed companies (and countries) develop a culture of care about their stockholders, employees, customers, environment, country, and neighbors, and become more successful than those who don't.

Finally, one sure sign of poor management is arrogance. There is a fine line between arrogance and self-confidence, but poor management will tend to talk down to others, play to their own egos, and imply the customers and/or competitors are less capable or qualified. If you run a company that is truly superior, you do not have to tell anyone; they all know it because it's obvious. If you have to say it, perhaps you do not think the others believe it (and perhaps you don't either). In a truly competitive world, it's very difficult to stay on top.

Growth and management Quality

If all this is true, how does poor management get to the top? I have not found the following conclusions recorded anywhere else, and have no way to verify the information. But I worked in Huntsville, Alabama in rocket and space programs from 1951 to 1992, and made the following observations.

During this period there were times of high growth, exceeding 20 percent per year. Some companies grew by a factor of ten in less than eight years. Adding and integrating employees, particularly at management levels, is not done as carefully at these times as it would be under lower risk conditions. As a result, the requirement of getting the job done promotes a lot of employees that normally would not have been advanced.

Once there, it is difficult to reduce or dismiss a loyal employee who helped the company when the times were tough. We tend to overlook certain irregularities, and compensate for poorer performances. In addition, during periods of high growth, it is not obvious who is efficient and who is not. High growth masks much inefficiency. Under the pressure of high growth, who would argue that a growth rate of 23 percent is bad and that it should have been 29 percent instead. During the latter part of the growth cycle, the legacy of poor management catches up and the organization becomes a highly political house of cards and eventually collapses.

If the company is well managed at the beginning of the rapid growth cycle, it may well go through the trauma of poorer management and recover. But during high growth cycles, it is very difficult to tell whether a company is well or poorly managed. During adverse times, it becomes obvious.

To provide some scale to address this problem, consider the following. During normal times, company growth would be in the range of 5 to 15 percent per year. At this rate, the top management has the time to cull out poor managers, teach the culture of superior performance, and maintain the constant improvement of corporate efficiency.

From revenue growth of 15 to 30 percent per year, efficiency gives away to expediency, and corners are cut. For periods of a year or two, this pace can be maintained and the company will continue without problems when normal growth returns. But if the high growth period extends for five or more years, the company will almost always go into a "flat spot" to get back to normal. If it doesn't, poorer management will gravitate to the top positions.

Growth rates of more than 30 percent per year will tend to develop a "war" culture where everything is overlooked except one particular goal. When this goal is eventually reached, the company will "tread water" until it returns to a culture of good or poor management. While this is going on, the company is subject to strong competitive pressures, and internal politics may prevent the purging of poor management. The poorer management will resort to unethical behavior to mimic the performance of good management and eventually cause the company to fail

Very well-managed companies like General Electric, Proctor and Gamble, and Coca Cola will be observed making three- to five-year spurts of growth and then hit a "flat spot" for a few years as they adjust to changing conditions. The high tech bubble of the 1996–2000 period is an example of companies not able to grow a management culture as fast as the revenue grew. As a result, risk was increased in these companies out of proportion to the rewards.

Annual Report

The board of directors represents the shareholders and has a fiduciary responsibility to them. Without a good board of directors, the stockholder does not have a chance.

Read the company philosophy as presented by the CEO in the annual report. It is important to learn about his character. The organization and presentation of the annual report tells more than the words. This is his chance to tell you what he's all about and to brag about the company's accomplishments. You can see what he wants you to know. If you didn't learn very much from the report, he probably didn't want you to know very much. Is there real meat in the report or is it a lot of smoke and mirrors? In particular look for any sign of arrogance, which is the first sign of deteriorating management quality. They will describe their product line and what they plan to do. Are you familiar with their products? Do you like them? Do you think you would like to work for that company? What kind of reputation does the company have? Perform an evaluation using a ranking number system of one to five, with one being excellent, three average, and five poor. Compare the information in the annual report of the target company to the that of the most significant competitor in its field, to the industry as compared to other industries in the market, and to the S&P 500. Use three (average) as the performance of the S&P 500.

Board of Directors

Look for diversity in the board of directors. Not the politically correct type of diversity, which refers to the number of racial minority members on the board. This refers to the composition of the board. Consider a variety of ages, usually from forty to seventy, with most being around sixty. We need excellent mature judgment, which is to be given to the Chief Executive Officer.

A significant number of younger "whiz kids" on the board predicts a risky environment. A lot of older ex-employees or retired officers portends a rubberstamp board. The biographical sketches of the board members will indicate their experience, education, and on how many other boards the individual serves. Many consider five to be the maximum number of boards a member should be allowed to attend. More than five will either will produce conflicts or reduce the amount of time the member has available for each company.

Boards of directors that include CEOs or officers of other successful companies in different industries predict a wealth of experience and lower risk. For example, consider a manufacturing company with board members such as a CEO of a large bank, a VP of a telecommunications company, a professor of a recognized university, an officer of a service company, a retired congressman or senator, other manufacturing company executives, and perhaps a union member. If some of these highly qualified individuals are racial minorities, so much the better.

It will be noted many boards contain political figures, retired military personnel, famous people, and/or their relatives. Check their credentials carefully so as to determine if they have the expertise to provide advice to top management or if they are window dressing meant to gain some political favor. Companies who use members as window dressing may well have an agenda other than the stockholders' welfare. However, many of these famous people are extremely talented and can provide judgment far in excess of their costs. Be careful in your evaluation, because the board of directors is your first and most important defense against fraud.

People write books to pass on experience, but there is no substitute for the wisdom of someone who has experienced this particular condition several times before. There is no substitute in the board room for "been there, done that." Top-notch board members should be independent, and one good sign of that is how secure are they in their other endeavors. You want a board member who is not afraid to quit if his or her standards are not met, or who has the stature to be able to fire the CEO if that becomes necessary.

When going through the biographical sketches, look for a wide variety and depth of experience in different industries, like banking, newspapers, universities, manufacturing, investment companies, basic materials, retailers, energy, healthcare, technology, and telecommunications. One company would not have all of these, but the idea is to have access to ideas and opinions from several different company executives. Successful cultures tend to replicate. Look for signs of how dependent or independent are the board members to the corporate officers. They are your representatives and they provide governance. If you have a problem with poor management, it starts here.

An example of a good board member would be Warren Buffet, America's second-wealthiest man. He gives lectures to various schools of business on management quality. The one conducted in North Carolina School of Business in 1995 was a particularly memorable event and is available from the Public Broadcasting System's online library. When you watch him talk to these business school graduates, it becomes easy to want him, or people like him, to run your company.

Buffet runs Berkshire Hathaway, a holding company which has grown somewhere north of 25 percent per year for thirty years. He buys and runs companies he understands; he doesn't get involved with companies he doesn't understand. His portfolio includes Coca-Cola, Gillette, insurance companies, candy companies, and furniture stores to name a few. He has fostered a culture of high-quality management. He plans to hold a company forever. He has developed a culture that will continue long after he's gone.

Compare him to his friend Bill Gates, the wealthiest man in America. His Microsoft has averaged a growth rate of over 61 percent per year for the 13.5 years between Sept 1986 and April 2000. Had the growth continued at this rate, it is estimated that Microsoft would have a market cap equal to U.S. GDP by 2006, and more the planet by 2008 (or 2009). This is obviously a ridiculous conclusion because growth-rate decreases as the company gets larger.

Microsoft has been extremely successful in developing and marketing software for the personal computer, and has been declared a monopoly by the courts. However, so far it has been a one-trick pony and has not been able to transfer that success into other fields. There are a couple of disturbing features of the management of Microsoft. At times they give the impression of arrogance, which is a predictor of problems. But more importantly, they have allowed the lawsuit concerning monopolistic practices to go on for so long. This distracts from their real purpose, which is to make money. They have $40 billion in cash that they can't seem to put to work effectively. The ROI leaves a lot to be desired.

Other companies in similar situations were ATT in 1980 and IBM a few years later. ATT was broken up and the regional telephone companies often called the baby bells prospered. IBM was not broken up but had to give away the PC business, including the software, to Microsoft. IBM went down for ten years before new management reoriented the company. Within five years more than 30 percent of their business was totally new.

EIGHTH ELEMENT—FUNDAMENTAL
ANALYSIS OF STOCKS

Fundamental analysis has been around for a long time. We use it every day when we buy groceries, a car, or a house. We develop an opinion as to the relationship between the price and the value of an item or service. We usually do this by comparing the item to an equivalent. Value is normally set at whatever someone would pay for that item; i.e., the price. However, value can also be established based on what the item will produce. The calculation of value based on what the item will produce is called fundamental analysis.

If the price is lower than the estimated (or comparative) value, we consider it to be a bargain and consummate the purchase. If not, we pass or buy another item. Many people do not do that and are willing to pay more for a certain brand because they believe it to be better. This price additive is called a franchise value.

A man named Benjamin Graham used a process called "Value Investing" after the crash of 1929. Value Investing is a strategy as well as a process. In 1934, Graham, who was called the father of value investing, taught at Columbia University. He wrote a book with David Dodd called *Security Analysis*, which described his technique of determining intrinsic value.

The Graham formula for determining intrinsic value, as described by Janet Lowe in her book *Value Investing made Easy*, is IV=E(2R+8.5)x4.4/Y where IV is intrinsic value, E is yearly earnings per share, R is rate of growth of earnings per share, and Y is the yield of the AAA corporate bond.

Improvements have been made to the process but the basic philosophy remains intact. One of the proponents of Value Investing is Warren

Buffet. One of his requirements is to understand what the company makes and how it is of value to society. He uses a method, which includes discounted cash flow to adjust for inflation. There are several very good books on this subject, including the one by Janet Lowe mentioned above.

The basic idea is to establish the value based on the company's ability to produce a profit as well as its ability to grow its earnings. The Return on Investment (ROI) is the usual criteria and is sometimes referred to as PE. If a person pays $20 per share for a stock that earns $1 per share in a year, the ROI is 5 percent and it has a PE of 20.

Another major factor for consideration is earnings growth (G). If the earnings is growing at the rate of 15 percent per year consistently, we say the G is 15. By dividing the PE by G we get the PEG ratio. For example if we divide 20 by 15 we get a peg ration of 1.3. A review of some historical data reveals the PEG ratio is related to the interest rate of the ten-year government bond. This ratio allows a rational comparison of several companies in a variety of industries. Please note Graham used "R" to denote earnings growth while today most analysts use "G" to represent the same item.

Traditionally, it was believed a "good" value was when the PE was equal to the growth rate. In other words, the PEG would be one. However, it was noted the PEs were much higher when interest rates were lower and very low PEs were noted at high interest rates. Empirical notations led to a conclusion that the PE ratio was most often at one when the bond was around 9 percent. Therefore, we can correct for interest rates by dividing 9 by the yield of the ten-year bond. If the ten-year bond was at 6 percent, then 9 divided by 6 would equal 1.5 as a typical PEG, and 1.3 would be a bargain PEG. PEs of 4 and up are not uncommon and require considerable faith because value may be hard to find.

Why doesn't everybody use this method? This is a logical question, and the answer comes in two parts. First, a very large number of people actually do use it. Second, it has one difficulty that is hard for a lot of (mostly impatient) people to resolve. When you find a bargain and buy it, you may have to wait a long time for others to recognize it. Many other people are still following the fads. To be a value investor requires patience. **It must be understood that people deciding to buy, is the force that makes the stock go up consistently** (not computers or analysts). If people have not recognized the value of the investment, then the price will languish. There is not the instant gratification as seen in momentum investing, neither is there the risk nor failure rates.

The lesson that needs to be learned repeatedly is that the reason for a company to exist is to produce a profit. There are nonprofit charitable organizations, but it is more than obvious they are not intended to produce a profit. All others are, and we all buy and sell on the expectations of this profit. The primary criteria for the ultimate decision is the return on investment.

Basics Rules

1. You (or anyone else) will never have ALL the information to make the best decision. But by making best use of what is available, you can increase probabilities substantially. You're making an **Opinion on Value.**
2. You are looking at past data, which tends to be a better predictor for well-managed companies, which are more stable.
3. You are trying to determine the future profit potential. The idea is to perform an objective analysis of historical data to determine the attributes of a company, and to compare these results with the results of other companies, industries, and markets. Although previous accomplishments tend to predict future performances, a prudent investor realizes all humans are prone to error.
4. Quality of information is paramount. It may take work to review a submission to the Security and Exchange Commission, but may be necessary. A few pieces of good data always outweigh a lot of poor data.

5. Quantity of information is not important. It is easy to rationalize that more information will result in a better answer. If you have four or five pieces of data that tell you it's a bad investment, you don't need to waste more time. You are trying to find a good reason to avoid this investment. If you find it, quit. That is why it is recommended to compare investments. If you have one good standard it's usually fairly easy to determine the second place finisher. This efficiency in time management is what you need to find in a company, and it will be easier to recognize it if you practice it yourself.

6. Good performance under adverse market conditions is of more value than good performance under better conditions. Thorough fundamental analysis helps to determine the most important feature of a company, which is the quality of company management.

7. Dividends are a sign that the management wants to share the profits of the company with the stockholders. It is unfortunate that this is one of the few countries that taxes stock dividends twice. The company pays tax on the profits before they are distributed, and then stockholders pay tax on those same profits when they received them.

Attributes by Which to Judge

Here are some of the major attributes to be developed for comparison:

Return on investment
Risk (Debt and debt ratios)
Enhancing shareholder value
Earnings and revenue growth rate
Response to adversity, markets, or economic developments
Quality of executive personnel
History of controlling the above attributes

Insider ownership (a high percentage is good)
Institutional ownership (average is best)

Pertinent Data

Some of the pertinent data used to evaluate (* dollars per share):
Price*
Earnings*
Earnings growth rate percent
Sales* (sometimes referred to as revenue)
Sales Growth Rate percent
Dividend*
Dividend Growth Rate (percent) (to determine consistency)
Book Value*
Equity Value*
Cash and Equivalents
Current Assets
Current Liabilities
Debt, long term
Debt, short term
EBITDA* (Earnings before interest, taxes, depreciation, and amortization)
Free Cash Flow*
Number of Shares

Items to Be calculated

P / E ratio,
PE / Growth (PEG)
Return on Assets
Return on Equity
Sales per share,
Sales growth rate

Total Return (dividends plus price growth) for 1 yr, 3 yr, 5 yr.
Long Term Debt
Ratio of Debt to Equity
Market capitalization (price per share times number of shares)
Current Ratio (Current Assets divided by Current Liabilities)
Working Capital (Current Assets minus Current Liabilities)
Compare Share Value to:
    To Book,
    To EBITDA,
    To Free Cash Flow
Compare Share Value to:
    Largest competitor(s)
    Sector Average
    S & P 500

The Analysis

The worksheet allows for tabulation of the data and efficient presentation. Most if not all of the information can be found in annual reports or on the Internet. Usually it is found under research or profile of the company. The calculations are simple but the analysis is the most important factor. It is necessary to do the calculations for the company and its competitor in order to provide a valid comparison. Not all of the information will be available (or appropriate) for the industry or the S&P 500.

Pay strict attention to the quality of information. Quite often, especially on Internet sites, the information is Pro forma and not GAAP (described later). This may not be the company's fault, but due to the analyst's agenda. It is worthwhile to determine the date and what is included as to operating earnings or all earnings. Comparison of information from several sources including the submissions to the government via the 10K reports allows one to determine which company is preferable.

In this analysis, think of yourself as an investigator like Sherlock Holmes or a Jessica Fletcher ("Murder She Wrote"). You are looking for anomalies, something that doesn't make sense, or for something wrong. For example if the company's PEG is 4, the its competitor's is 2.5 and the S&P is 2, then you need to dig deeply to make sure that company is worth the extra price. Lower risk often commands a higher price. But when a blue chip company in business for a hundred years has a lower PEG than an IPO (Initial Public offering), then the IPO is not a prudent investment unless the circumstances are extreme.

Many times a company has had a high PE because the growth is high, but later when the growth dries up, the PE remains high for quite a while before it comes back to normal. This company is considered overvalued during that period of time. The traders who short stocks (see Glossary), will force the price down eventually. Also, many times a PE will be very low because most investors have sold out because future earnings are projected to drop.

It is very important to include all the information. For example, today (March 2002) MSFT carries a PE of 55 TTM (Trailing Twelve Months) and the earnings growth rate is expected to be under 7 percent this year. If you compare today's price ($60) with what they are expected to earn next year, the PEG is 7.8. The earnings for next year are not expected to increase substantially. This price is too high and eventually it will adjust to reflect the present performance. The past growth rates of 30 to 50 percent per year are still holding the price up.

The use of Pro forma reports can easily cause misrepresentation of the analysis. Pro forma means to carry out in a perfunctory manner, or as a formality. It is an advanced statement when all accurate information is not available. For example, when two companies merge, the organization of the balance sheets may not be completed in time for the annual report. An advanced pro forma report is issued and corrected later, including losses not previously reported. However, many of the newer high tech companies have been using this technique all the time to report results, then when they correct to reflect true amounts, the performance is considerably lower. The final report, however, does not usually get as much attention. This deception was only a part of the Enron problem. The other part was outright lying by management.

There is a great deal more information than necessary available. Some people tend to saturate themselves with copious quantities of data. All you need is enough to make a good decision. As soon as you find a reason to reject the stock, it may be wise to quit and spend time on other studies. A positive answer takes a lot more time than a negative one. You are looking for a true assessment of the value of the company, which will predict future earning with a reasonably high level of probability.

Much information provides the same conclusion in a slightly different manner. Yes, it reinforces your conclusion but will not essentially change your mind. Please understand this is not really engineering calculations. If you compare two companies and find one 10 or 20 percent better than another, you can make an informed decision. To analyze further and determine that one was actually 9.6 percent better rather than 10 percent better is not really worth the extra effort. If you find one 1.5 percent better, it is essentially a toss up. Although buying both would cost more brokerage fees, it would reduce volatility. Efficient use of your time and resources will help you to recognize companies that also do the same. Efficient companies usually win.

Worksheet for Fundamental Analysis

The worksheet shown as Table 1 is provided as an example of a minimum effort. The number of data lines may be expanded for more energetic investors. Information for all blocks may not be available, but a prudent investor will fill in as many as reasonably possible. Get the information for the corporation to be investigated (Corp), the major competitor (Comp), the industry or sector, and the S&P 500 which represents the market. The Dow Jones Industrials may also be used, but the S&P 500 is a more accurate representation of the entire market. Much of the information is available and often available on the Internet with the calculations completed.

Research is available through online brokers, Yahoo.com, ClearStation.com and StockCharts.com. Free cash flow is available from ValuePro.net. Other information is available from annual reports, and Free Edgar hosted by the government at sec.gov. For ease of comparison, most items are shown in dollars per share, as a percentage ratio or numerical rank. Others are in total dollars but will be used in calculation to give ratios. Comparing PE and PEG ratios provide a good perspective.

When evaluating company management use a numerical rank where a scale of one to five is used with one being best and five being the worst. Look at the biographical sketches for each member of the board of directors and compare the strength experience of one board to the other. Use subjective judgment to determine if one is substantially better than the other. Give a score of four to the lesser and two to the more experienced board. After you look at several boards, you will be able to estimate the median or number three position. Charm and articulation have no value in this area. The basic question is "will this person protect my life savings?" For the Sector or market assign the average number of three.

Table 1	Fundamantal Analysis Work Sheet			Date_____
Data	Corp	Comp	Industry/Sector	S & P 500
Price $				
Earnings $				
Earn Grwth %				
Div Yld %				
Price/Sales P/S				
Sales Grwth %				
EBIDTA $				
Cash Flow $/Share				
PE Ratio $/Share				
PEG $/Sh/% Ern Gr.				
Ret Assets %				
Ret Equity %				
Total Ret 1yr. %				
Total Ret 3yr %				
Total Ret 5yr. %				
Debt/Equity %				
Current Ratio %				
Board (***)				
Company Phil (***)				
Inside owner (***)				
Institutional own (***)				
(***) numerical rank from 1-5 with 1 being best				

Do the same with company philosophy. Are they minding the business of protecting my money, or do they have some other agenda? It is not unreasonable to pay a lot for superior skills; however, it is unreasonable to pay for lack of performance. If you discover that situation, it is more prudent to sell or not buy, whatever is appropriate.

A higher than average amount of inside ownership would warrant a higher assigned value, or a less desirable circumstance. The reason being that the inside owners would have better control of the board of directors. A higher than average institutional ownership should also make one cautious. If a large institution decides to drop a company, it can be very bad for the price of a stock. In past years it was a reasonable assumption that a large institutional ownership would guarantee someone independent checking up on the management. But the Enron debacle puts that concept to rest. It is reasonable to assume that an undervalued company (that is as yet undiscovered) would not have a large institutional following.

Some people like to add the numbers and pick the one with the best showing. But remember that a large number of these values are subjective, and it is not prudent to consider it a scientific analysis. I do not like to use this technique because not all of the items are of equal weight. Think of it as a job interview. Would you like to have these people work for you? Do you trust them? Make a gut feeling evaluation on how you would like to associate with them.

I would consider the order of importance to be:
1. Integrity,
2. Attitude toward developing a viable culture within the company,
3. Protection of important assets including the customers and employees,
4. Consistency of earnings growth compared to the market's growth, and
5. The growth rate of earnings.

Others may select a different set of criteria and order of importance. However, by using the worksheet and looking for these qualities in a comparison mode, it is not too difficult to weed out the weaker companies.

There are managers who can perform well over the short term. However, to perform over the long term is much more difficult, and also to perform well in adverse conditions requires superior people. When you buy stock in a company, you are buying (hiring) the management. The worksheet is not to quantify the assets of the company but to quantify the quality of management.

NINTH ELEMENT—TECHNICAL ANALYSIS OF STOCKS

A word of caution must be presented. **There is no Holy Grail.** By that I mean there is no one single indicator that will guarantee success in investing. Most indicators work under certain conditions, and all indicators fail under certain conditions. The trick, if there is one, is to find out which work under which conditions.

Technical analysis of stock trends is not a science where a specific formula will render an accurate result. The field of science has developed accurate predictions as to the boiling point of water, the load capability of a beam, and other physical factors that can be established and easily reproduced.

However, people buy stocks, and the resulting price movements are subject to the wills, desires, feelings, and impulses of the participants. Probability, perception, anticipation, and the emotional gut feeling play a very important role in the movement of stock prices. Add panic, and you have a typical market condition. Technical analysis attempts to predict, at a reasonable level of probability, the future stock price movement due to all of these actions.

It is appropriate to mention that this document does not contain much information for the trader. Stock and options trading is a sophisticated technique that has several books dedicated solely to the subject. The following information is presented to allow the average investor to appreciate the venue of the trader who makes buy and sell decisions primarily based on technical analysis.

History

In 1884, Charles Dow, publisher of the *Wall Street Journal*, made up an average of eleven stocks, nine of which were railroad companies. He recorded the fluctuations of this average, and concluded its movement represented the judgment of the buying public, and tended to predict to some degree future stock price activity. It was called the Dow theory and did seem to give an advantage to those who used the system.

It was constantly refined and by the 1920s Robert Schabacker, editor of *Forbes* magazine developed a set of "signals". John Magee, a graduate of MIT, joined his brother-in-law, Robert D. Edwards, in 1942, and together they added additional analysis. Their book, *Technical Analysis of Stock Trends*, first published in 1948 and now in its seventh edition (1997), is considered the bible of technical analysis. It is the basis of most of the information in this chapter. Its seven hundred pages will provide you with more than you will want to know about technical analysis. Since then, many additions to stock trend analysis has been developed, most notably a program by Don Worden called TC 2000, which is available to the computer literate public at modest prices. Most of the information presented herein is derived from Dow, Magee, and Worden.

Basics

The primary observations by Charles Dow are:
1. The price of a stock is due to the buying and selling forces, and represents true value at that point in time.
2. A major trend is presumed to continue until there is clear evidence of a reversal.
3. It's possible to form opinions from market activity that have a high probability of success.

Others have added phenomena such as the effect of volume on stock price action. Abnormally high or low volume during certain price movements reveals significant information as to changes in price trends. Recognizing trend changes is perhaps the most important feature of technical analysis.

To assist in recognizing trend changes, another aspect is the ability to evaluate the introduction of "smart money". Logic seems to indicate that those who have the ability to purchase or sell stocks in large blocks (like ten thousand shares or more) will have more incentive, capability, and resources to develop better information. For every seller there is a buyer. But if a person is buying ten thousand shares from sellers who are predominately one hundred or one thousand share sellers, the event is described as "the stock is moving into smart hands." The probability is that the stock will rise. Within a day's trading of a specific stock, there is always an average ratio of large block to small block investors. When this ratio changes significantly from the norm, a conclusion can be drawn as to whether smart money is getting in or out of a position. However, please remember most smart money is from mutual funds, and as of this time (2001) the average age of a mutual fund manager is less than twenty-nine. On occasion smart money does not appear to be very smart. Buyer beware.

Most technical analysis is presented in charts because it is easier to evaluate a graphic representation of several interacting complex features. These charts are usually made up of a series of vertical lines, each of which represent a specific time, such as one day or one week, etc. A quick glance can show the high and low for that period and a short horizontal line will show the close. Over a period of time, these vertical lines form a wavy horizontal band indicating characteristics of a war being conducted between the buyers who believe the stock is going up versus the sellers who think the stock is going down.

Please be aware that the probabilities normally associated with this type of analysis are NOT of the engineering levels as in two and three sigma limits (95 and 99 percent). [Sigma refers to standard deviation, a notation in statistical analysis] It is with considerable good fortune the expectations

MAY rise to one sigma or 66 percent. I repeat, technical analysis is an art, not a science.

Trend Analysis

Imagine a chart where the price of a stock is rising over a period of time. Seldom is it a straight line. The price responds to news stories, external events, and factors sometimes not really associated with the stock. Fear and greed are two highly emotional forces which demonstrate major effect. A positive report will often make it rise considerably, after which it stalls. Figure 1 illustrates a typical price action. The vertical line represents the high and low for that particular day and the little tick attached to the right side of the line is the closing price.

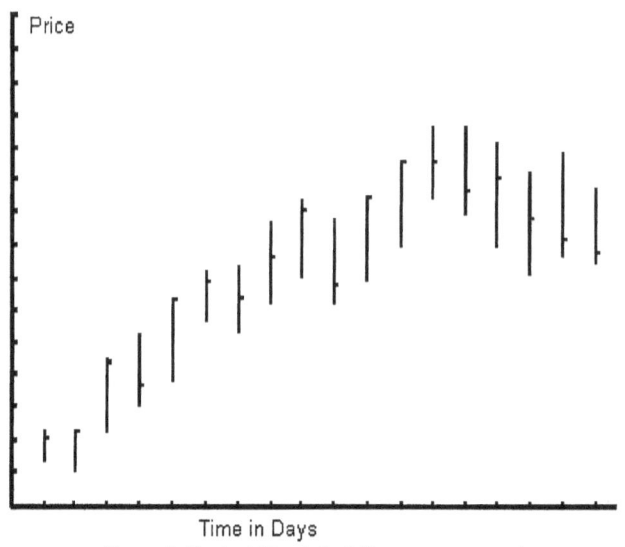

Time in Days
Figure 1 Typical Stock Activity

After a price rise, some feel the price has gone too high and will soon go down so they sell. Others hold on. As the price increases, a straight line is drawn touching the bottoms of the daily prices. As long as the prices stay above the line, the trend continues until there is enough sellers. This will provide clear evidence that the uptrend is broken as shown in Figure 2. The character of the trend has changed (as per Magee and Edwards) when the total activity and closing price is below the trend line. and a new assessment must be made as to the future price action. During a downtrend, the reverse is true and the trend line touches the tops of the daily lines. However, the essential feature of the analytical process is to recognize the change of character and to take appropriate action.

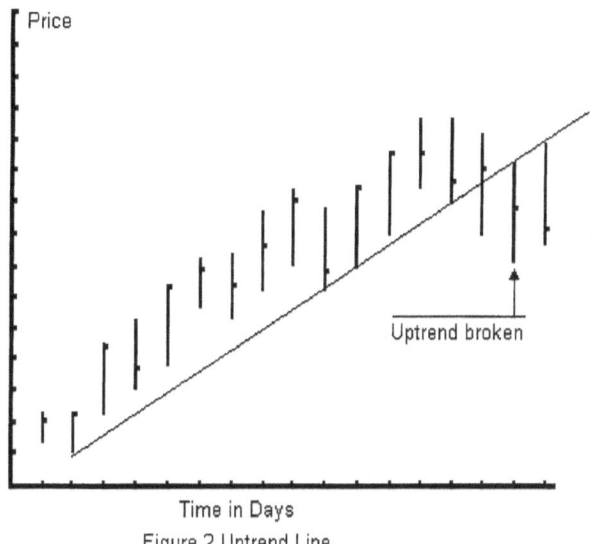

Figure 2 Uptrend Line

With the advent of the computer, it is easier and sometimes more significant to use several moving averages. Figure 3 shows the same daily activity with five and ten day moving averages. When the averages cross, it is a signal that the character has changed.

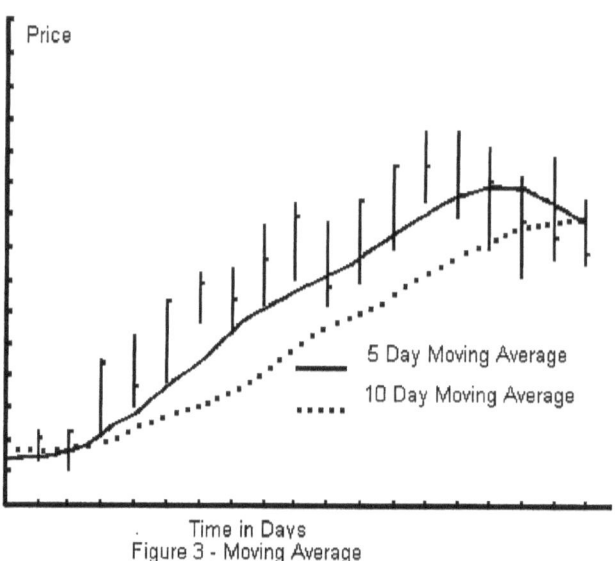

Figure 3 - Moving Average

Note in Figure 3 that the signal is one day later than the signal given in Figure 2. By changing the time period, the sensitivity of response time can be changed. Some technicians use three- and seven-day moving averages instead of five and ten. When trading, however, too short a time period will add confusion with respect to normal daily volatility. Others wish to determine longer trends to avoid being whipsawed in and out of the investments, and pick moving averages up to two hundred days.

The trend is sometimes horizontal for extended periods of time. These are considered base formations and are considered strong positions if they stay around a narrow price range for an extended period of time. A stock may rise and fall back to this level repeatedly, as shown in Figure 4.

If this base is below the price level it is called a support level. The rationale is that some investors had owned the stock and sold before the rise. When it came back down, many of these people now have the opportunity to get back into the investment. Therefore, there is a built-in demand in this price range.

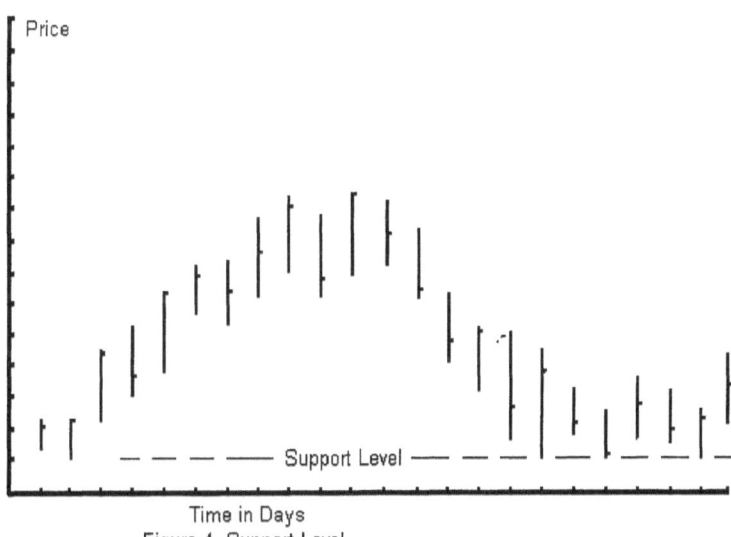

Time in Days
Figure 4 Support Level

If the stock trades below this base, it is called a resistance level because some people bought the stock earlier and it went down. Now that it has gone back to that price, they want out. There is a built-in supply at this price.

A breakthrough of a support or resistance level should be regarded as a significant event. Usually the trend will continue to another support or resistance level. Many times, these are the "stopping points" where a change trend occurs.

A breakout from a resistance level, support level, uptrend line or downtrend line is called a violation. This breakthrough may indicate a need to sell, or just to make a change in the trend line. The trader's dilemma is to decide how much profit must be lost before the sell decision is executed.

Every successful technician needs to become a chart reader. Reading the chart is an art more than a science, because the chart portrays the decision-making process of the investors. These decisions comprise of some ratio of rational to irrational (or emotional) decisions. This ratio varies considerably over time. The most disturbing and traumatic period is during panic selling. Panic buying is sometimes seen and described as irrational exuberance. Fear and greed overwhelms the senses and produces these responses.

Volume is an added dimension to the analysis. An uptrend on increasing volume is bullish. An uptrend on contracting volume is a bearish sign. A downward breakout on increased volume is usually a bad sign and a strong sell indicator. As the prices decline, the price predictability becomes more difficult as gurus predict the worst is over and advise that "now is the time to get in," although the fundamentals continue to be bad. However, low volume at the bottom of a downward trend may not indicate anything significant.

Initially at the trend change into a bear market there is increased volume, but over a longer downtrend, the price is dropping because of lack of buyers. After the panic sellers get out, the remaining owners prefer to sit and wait it out. In long-term bear markets, the volume tends to get lower as price decreases and ends in what is referred to as capitulation, or giving up. The market becomes boring and no one seems interested.

Gradually the volume increases as the stock moves from weaker hands to stronger hands. Speculation decreases, and predictability of future prices becomes easier. This Increasing volume at the end of a long downtrend is a bullish sign.

Some software is very sophisticated and will have additional boxes below the chart so other indicators show the responses at the same time as the upper bar chart. Using multiple indicators is a valuable way to confirm conclusions and increase the probability of success.

Now we can add statistical bands to the moving averages and establish overbought and oversold indicators. Markets seldom move in nice clean lines, but rather in fits and starts, responding to any fad or fancy. The movements make it appear like a turn is just around the corner. The great bear market of 2000–2002 in Nasdaq gave four sell signals and three buy signals before it completed it's 55 percent drop. There were plenty of signals and ample time.

It is of considerable value for an average investor to learn even a modicum of technical analysis so as to evaluate the performance of the gurus and pundits. Almost all investors want to hear about the end of a bear market, so the advisors happily comply. But the truth is of more value than casting good money after bad.

In addition to the chart, there are many other technical analysis techniques, two of which include the Fibonacci retracement curves and candlestick charts. It is worthwhile to be cautious. The key feature of all types of analysis is to learn when it applies and when it doesn't.

Below are listed some indicators used in technical analysis.

Moving Average: A moving average is used to smooth trends. A ten-day moving average adds together the last ten days, divides by ten and plots that number at the ten-day mark. For the next day it adds the eleventh day, subtracts the first day, and divides by ten. This process continues, forming a trend line on the graph. If two lines are constructed using two different time frames (i.e. ten days and fifty days), they will run parallel if the trend continues. When the lines cross, it signals a trend change and prompts a buy or sell activity.

Envelope Channel: Two lines are formed, one above and one below the moving average and can be set at the discretion of the user. Usually it is useful at one sigma (standard deviation). It is a good indicator of overbought and oversold conditions, as well as confirming trend changes.

Bollinger Bands: Developed by John Bollinger, the indicator is essentially an envelope channel using volatility of prices as its basis of calculations. This tends to reduce false breakouts.

Volume Bars: The volume is plotted each day with the color changed to register whether the close was up, neutral, or down. Usually red indicated down, yellow neutral, and green up. It is easy to see rising red bars as a potential sell signal and trend change.

Stochastics: It measures where a stock is trading within the recent price range and uses price velocity. It is an overbought/oversold indicator. A moving average of the stochastic is a basis for buy and sell signals.

MACD: Moving Average Convergence Divergence was created by Gerald Appel to produce trading signals. It is easy to interpret and helps to identify trends more efficiently. It consists of three exponential moving averages and is displayed as two lines. As one moves through the other it produces a buy or sell signal. It also can be seen as a histogram.

RSI: There are a lot of Relative Strength Indicators available. Some compare the price of the stock to an index or another stock. But one type, Wilders, compares it to itself and indicates overbought and oversold conditions.

It's All About Money

Trend analysis provides an inkling as to where the money is going. However, there are several indicators that provide a better analysis of smart money. Each one looks at the problem a little differently. They include but are not limited to the following:

Money Stream: A proprietary technique developed by Don Worden. As with other similar indicators, it looks for divergences. The slope of the money stream regression line compared to the slope of the price line is a good indicator. There are some competitors called Money Flow.

On Balance Volume: Developed by Joe Granville quite a while ago, it looks at the problem a little differently. It adds total volume on up days and subtracts total volume on down days. A rising OBV is bullish.

Time Segmented Volume: Another proprietary indicator by Worden. It is an oscillator which is calculated by comparing various time segments of price and volume. It tends to display accumulation or buying pressure (up), and distribution or selling pressure (down).

Balance of Power: Another Worden proprietary indicator is intended to indicate the systematic accumulation or distribution of a stock. It shows supply and demand rather than where the money is coming from.

Final Observations

This is only a sample of some technical indicators. Each has considerable more influence than the brief description shows. By using many indicators, the investor has the opportunity to see the problem from different viewpoints, thereby increasing the probability of a true conclusion. However, one must be cautious using similar indicators like RSI, MACD, and Stochastics, believing they are totally independent. It is best to use both money and volume indicators.

With the use of modern software and a good computer, an investor can scan all 7300 stocks within minutes using their investment criteria and have a high probability of making a successful trade. Is this too good to be true? The answer is "yes" if a person reads too much into the process. Consider the problems with too much technical analysis:

1. The Quality of emotionally engendered information has a rapid decay rate. An overwhelming buy or sell signal is good for only a few days at most. You are only measuring what people think of that stock at that time. Fads change rapidly. This is not a long-term investment tool.

2. It does not have a reasonably good capability to pick well-managed companies. That must be done through the judgment process under fundamental analysis. The chart can easily mislead.

3. Although It cannot anticipate other factors, including market forces, macroeconomics, or politics, it can display when many of the investors believe these other factors are affecting the stock.

4. It assumes all information is true and accurate, and is not capable of assessing the quality of information. This alone is perhaps the weakest point of technical analysis.

But it does have one over riding feature equally useful to the trader and long-term investor. It identifies impending disasters beforehand by recording the exit of the most knowledgeable early birds, privy to inside or yet to be distributed information. These early warning signs usually favors one's financial health.

Tenth Element—Macroeconomics

Macroeconomics addresses the behavior of large economic entities such as countries and continents. It analyzes unemployment, gross domestic product, etc. It is used to appraise the condition of the large-scale economy, and how it affects our country, our company, and our pocketbook.

Some of these conditions have a positive or negative effect on an investment. They include: catastrophes (like earthquakes, hurricanes, droughts, volcanoes, tidal waves), wars and strife (declared or not), a worldwide economic depression or inflation, embargos, politics, environmental changes, and peace.

The problem with catastrophes is that money is being spent to get back where you started, rather than to create an advance in society. A particular calamity may be confined to one country, but it can easily have global macroeconomic effects by disrupting patterns of commerce.

The large majority of investment decisions are made based on fundamental or technical analysis of the equity in question. These two types of analysis tend to predict with a reasonable level of confidence what the probable value of the investment will become at sometime in the future if all other things are equal. The fundamental analysis reveals the past value and profit-making trends of the organization. Technical analysis presents the public's reaction to the company's activities as shown by price action.

However, macroeconomics affects the price of any investment, and is outside of the control of the company or stockholders. A prudent investor will keep a wary eye on these factors, to minimize any potential negative effects. Investors can feel helpless as they see their investment wither due to these factors, even though the fundamental performance is acceptable.

In order to understand these factors it is necessary to understand the relationship between the effects of profit and growth. All economic growth comes from a portion of profits. Profit is defined as the amount of money left over after all costs and taxes are paid. This profit may go to the stockholders or the owner(s), or be invested by the company itself. It will be spent on many activities over and over again, but eventually a certain amount will be saved and reinvested in some enterprise. This investment will create jobs and seek improved productivity for the purpose of making more profit. Faster, better, cheaper is the goal of those who want to make more profit. Adam Smith, in his famous eighteenth century classic *Wealth of Nations*, provides an excellent discussion on the invisible hand, which causes economic growth and improves the standard of living.

Certain needed activities do not improve productivity and in some instances retard growth. These include maintaining prisons, law enforcement activities, military defense systems, and insurance programs. However, these activities are necessary to minimize losses that would be incurred if these systems were not available. Governmental activities do not (nor ever have) created jobs. It redistributes jobs by taking money (which would have been a job for somebody) away from an individual or company and replaces it with a job somewhere else.

Barron's (the business and financial weekly newspaper) published a fine article in one of their June 2001 issues on "Macroeconomics, Market forces, and Company Management". This presentation includes some of their information and expands the considerations.

Although the money paid into insurance companies is invested in productive enterprises, eventually all of it is spent on repaying losses (except for the profit of the insurance company). The insurance process tends to spread out the effect of these losses. It includes the expenditures as the regular cost of doing business.

Wars result in spending money for war materials, which, granted are necessary for survival, but do not increase the standard of living. The destruction caused by war substantially reduces the standard of living in that area. However, it must be recognized that the study of war history reveals that since the technology of the victors is generally superior, their culture usually improves the economy of the vanquished, but this improvement is not commensurate with the destruction. The threat of war is also expensive. There will always be extremists, and therefore the threat of war.

Inflation and depressions are imbalances in financial infrastructures. Most of the time they are caused by political decisions, inadequate controls by the financial regulators, or lack of knowledge about market forces. The "Asian Contagion" of the late 1990s is a perfect example where a large number of investors lost considerable amounts of money because of inadequate risk assessment.

There will always be fleecers and fleecees, but improved information distribution and information quality helps to avoid the negative effect. Truthful information tends to reveal the hidden political agenda and managerial incompetence of the fleecers. As our experience increases, the negative factors of imbalanced financial structures are being mitigated. But risky financial structures need to be considered.

Embargos and wars are restraint of trade issues, which are political in nature and result in overpricing due to the inability of people to take advantage of the low-cost producer. The oil embargos of the 1970s resulted in a catastrophic economic effect worldwide. Its final effect was to reduce the power of OPEC. The U.S. embargo (1978) against the Soviet Union because of the Afghanistan invasion punished our farmers and had minimal effect on Russia. The embargo of Cuba (1960's to present) has had the opposite effect from destroying Castro's power. Embargos are political decisions instituted when a country feels it cannot compete openly.

Negative environmental effects have not (yet) reached macroeconomic proportions. Considerable effort and concern is being expended to prevent this condition because of the potential problem of reaching the point of no return. Some of the near misses include the Chernobyl nuclear accident in Russia, the Exxon Valdese tanker problem, the Three Mile Island accident, and acid rain in U.S. and Canada. Just over the horizon are problems with global warming and the reduction of the ozone layer over Antarctica. In spite of all the rhetoric, these problems have yet to be clearly defined and solutions determined. But the consequences of an adverse environmental condition could have enormous effects on an investor, as could the effect of squandering large amounts of capital on phantom solutions. Politicians have a long record of such squandering, sometimes called "pork barrel politics."

Peace is the condition that has the most positive effect on the world's population. The net effect is that taxes are lower, fewer resources are wasted and more are devoted to increasing productivity. This results in added discretionary income, a higher standard of living, the creation of jobs and distribution of wealth. Wealth distribution has proven to be a positive effect on the world's economy. Those attempts at bailing a country out of financial problems usually fail because the rich and powerful of that country get it and squander it. The most effective method of wealth distribution is to allow free trade where poor (or devastated) countries can take advantage of their only resource (cheap labor) and make a profit.

Henry Ford taught the cogent lesson in wealth distribution in the early 1900s when he paid his workers the unheard sum of $5 a day. Many other car companies tried to stop him because the economic mantra of the time was to pay as low a wage as possible and keep the labor just above subsistence wages. The workers at U.S. Steel during this time were making fourteen cents per hour while working twelve hours per day ($1.68 per day), and had to work seven days per week without overtime pay. Ford made up the difference by inventing mass production. He created a financially strong middle class that could afford more cars.

The second chapter of the wealth distribution story was accomplished via the Marshall plan after World War 2. The U.S. provided capital and markets for many war torn countries, and those who took advantage of it soon prospered. The Eastern block countries that retained a controlled society remained poor for decades.

Any astute student of the last five thousand years of recorded history (Durant's *Story of Civilization*), will realize the highest standards of living were attained by those civilizations who practiced free trade. Several of these civilizations were successful for many centuries and compare favorably to ours. These include Egypt (3000 BC), Babylonia (2000 BC), Phoenicia (1200 BC), Greece (800 BC), Rome (1 BC), China (700), the Muslim world (900), and Europe (1700).

Those who decry free trade and complain about globalization are doing civilization a disservice. Recorded history shows no instance where restraint of trade for any extended period of time has improved the standard of living for the general population. It has often rewarded the few at the expense of the majority. The Soviet experience is an example. However, from this example the reader is cautioned not to conclude that a country that practices socialism cannot be competitive. Sweden and France are two examples of successful economies with socialistic polices. It is the restraint of trade in a controlled society that is damaging.

ELEVENTH ELEMENT—MARKET FORCES

Market forces are usually confined to one country and are mostly influenced by local political and monetary (economic) policies. Of great importance is the financial infrastructure, liquidity of the market, and transparency. Major issues include interest rates, tax burdens, education and skill level of the work force, information distribution, and transportation costs to available markets.

The effect of these major issues on the profitability of companies operating in a given market is easy to recognize. If I have to pay less interest on my capital, I can buy newer and more productive equipment cheaper than my competitor. If I pay fewer taxes I can sell my product at a lower price and retain more profit and upgrade my equipment. If my workforce is more educated and skilled, they are more flexible and are further down the learning curve; i.e., more productive. If I'm close to my market, I'll pay less transportation cost and have more funds for better equipment.

It must be realized that the most important fact of economic life is that the war is always won in the long run by the low-cost producer; that is low cost for the same product. One extremely difficult task in investing is to compare identical items (apples to apples and oranges to oranges). The same problem exists when comparing companies.

Controlled markets can produce enormous advantages for short periods of time. The Japanese economy is a good example. During the 1970s and early 1980s they had a boom for several reasons, including their ability to use more automated machinery than the U.S. could, and the fact they did not have to pay any tax on products shipped overseas. However, although they generated great amounts of capital, they would not open their markets.

At that time, nine out of the ten of the largest banks in the world were Japanese. The boom collapsed in 1988 when others caught up in price and quality. They moved their factories to North America rather than allow free trade. Their economy went into a depression that has continued for thirteen years. This protectionism has produced devastating results, with their stock market dropping from thirty-five thousand to twelve thousand. Several of their banks went out of business, and only one is in the top ten.

As with the U.S. economy during the Great Depression, the Japanese market forces created by political expediency and lack of leadership devastated the economy. Governments and markets with the lowest cost to the corporation will grow and flourish, providing the best return on the investment for the shareholders. Certain political elements in some markets eschew even the concept of profits and consider them evil. However, there is a wealth of information to demonstrate that improved standards of living are only due to profits or increases in discretionary income.

A good example is shown by India and China. India formed a democratic government in 1949, but selected a socialistic governmental-controlled society. Feeding the population was a problem for many years. At about 1989 they changed to a free and competitive market and have been growing at approximately 8 percent per year since. Many things are expensive but food is pretty much available to all at reasonable prices. They have the largest community of software developers in the world. Everybody is a capitalist.

China is not totally democratic and market free but is moving strongly in that direction. Their economic growth rate is similar to India's. They have taken advantage of Chinese businessmen living in other countries. At night Shanghai is barely discernable from a typical western city. These two countries will become superpowers in the not too distant future. Their markets have become unfettered compared to a few years ago.

PUT IT ALL TOGETHER

It is important for the prudent investor to know where he or she fits into the financial community. To do this one should apply **common sense** and accept the **responsibility** to develop the applicable **strategies** for financial health. Without careful application of these first three elements, other efforts are a waste of time. The strategy needs to be addressed only a few times during the lifetime of the average person.

Regardless whether a person is a passive or active investor, they should take extra caution to develop the **Quality of Information** that will be used to make decisions. Comparisons of different information sources will illustrate inconsistencies and areas of caution. The amount of deceptive information is probably minimal, but the information we need to be especially careful of comes from sources that do not do their homework nor possess acceptable set of values. Truth is your greatest protection.

By adhering to the cautions of the **Legends of Wall Street,** investors can lower risk by avoiding pitfalls discovered by others. After you make a decision as to a particular investment, filter it through the Legends of Wall Street. Quite often it will prevent an investor from replacing common sense with enthusiasm.

The investor needs to know the effect of the **Gurus** just once to prevent their adverse effects from obstructing his financial growth. All recommendations and observations are not created equal. It is your responsibility to determine which are best.

Investors can keep out of trouble by learning how to determine the **Quality of Company Management.** When you buy a stock, you are not buying a software company or automobile maker. You are buying management judgment. High-quality management will develop a culture of integrity and long-term success. The crooks are selling short-term success for their own benefit.

Any successful crook does not look like a crook. In order to have any record of success, he must be charming, articulate, and claim to have your interest at heart. Good looks also help. You will see this in politics as well as in business. As the famous bank robber Willy Sutton replied when asked why he robs banks, "because that's where the money is." The Security and Exchange Commission and law enforcement as well as the stock exchanges go to extraordinary lengths to provide protection. But ultimately it's your responsibility to learn the truth. Your safest ticket to financial success is to buy companies that have a culture of high-quality management.

The prudent passive investor will select a broker or fund to manage his or her portfolio, which has been selected based on the appropriate strategy. He or she will inform and keep informed those who are assisting in the decision-making process. He will look over their shoulders at intervals to insure compliance with the strategy.

The active investor will select a stock by the use of **Fundamental Analysis** as it relates to, and in concert with, the **Macroeconomic Conditions** and existing **Market Forces**. Generally he will pick a low-risk company doing something he understands, with high-quality experienced management. He will hold onto the stock until there is an indication of an adverse management change. Depending on conditions, he may upgrade his portfolio to recognize changes in macroeconomics and market forces. Otherwise he holds onto his positions.

He will use **Technical analysis** to assess advantageous entry and exit points, and to provide early warning signs of future problems with the fundamentals of the company or its relationship with existing conditions.

The astute investor will use all of these elements much like an artist uses different colors of paint or a composer uses different instruments. But above all, common sense is the most important tool. It is worthwhile to repeat the ultimate goal, which is to develop a productive teddy bear portfolio. That is the kind you can sleep with at night.

EPILOGUE

This document was started in about 1992 and was essentially completed in mid 2001. However, events changed rapidly and new circumstances required additional attention. There was one event recently that needs special attention. That is the Enron event. Although not really unique, it is of great rarity to have a large corporation cheat on a large scale, have its deception covered up by the board, which were party to the deception, and compounded by the auditors.

This process was experienced in the 1920s with some frequency. It was part of the reason for the huge bubble and subsequent crash of the 1930s. Companies were reporting profits but were not in fact making money. The true intrinsic value of the stocks did not warrant the prices of 1929. But very few knew it. In all probability, the lows of the early 30s were also not warranted. The catastrophe of the 1920s created the Securities and Exchange Commission (SEC).

Today we see this in penny stocks and very small companies where just a few people are needed to maintain the deception. The public is not usually affected and a few gamblers go home broke. The Enron catastrophe required a large number of people to orchestrate the deception, the board of directors to sanction it, and the auditors to comply. Because of this activity, about eighty thousand Enron employees, fifty thousand Anderson employees, and many thousands of stockholders have had their lives disrupted in a major way. The innocents pay for the crime.

In all probability, some drastic regulations will be put in place to prevent this from happening in the future. They were not making money, but hid that fact from the public. People complain that they did not pay taxes. True; they didn't owe any. This is an important lesson. If a company pays dividends and income taxes, they're making money. It will take time to play this thing out, but some people should go to jail.

The first line of defense is the integrity of the top management. The talented ones usually are good and honest. The less talented tend to compensate by cutting corners. Often charm is substituted for talent.

The second line of defense against a crooked management is the board of directors. There are some who believe (incorrectly) that the stockholders should not establish pay and other rights of management. All of management serves at the pleasure of the stockholders. The board represents the stockholders first. They have a responsibility to the stockholders. There are a lot of companies whose board does not represent the stockholders. Owning these is a threat to your financial health.

Third line is the auditor. I have no pity for any Anderson employee who lost his or her job because of a mistake by someone else. There is a basic fact of life: bad companies get punished and good ones (usually) don't. I got punished because a broker did not know what he was doing. This happens all the time. Try to buy companies who have integrity and make a profit. Try to work for the same kind of companies. If you work for a company that is arrogant and cuts corners, get another job.

But the troubles of Enron could have been predicted much earlier. The technical analysis showed a lot of the big players were on their way out in June 2001. The fundamental analysis had a huge divergence in that it showed a profit, but there was a negative cash flow. Divergences eventually get resolved. There were a lot of signs but most people did not want to believe them.

If a person does not want to believe, then there is nothing you can do about it. We can only help those who will listen.

Because of the Enron scandal, many good companies were heavily scrutinized and the price of the stock was punished. They had to work very hard and every item was reviewed. We don't feel sorry for those companies either. It made them better and they will stay on top. Live with it.

The war on terrorism was not originally a consideration, but it is definitely a macroeconomic effect. We will have to spend a great deal on security that otherwise would have gone to improving productivity. The growth rate of the world's economy will slow because of this war. The war could last over a decade. Every forty year period seems to have a depression. There was one in 1930, one in 1970, so there could be one in 2010, give or take a few years. Be prepared.

GLOSSARY

AAII: American Association of Individual Investors. A non-profit organization dedicated to helping the individual investor to develop skills in investing in stocks and mutual funds.

Active Investor: One who actively manages his or her own portfolio.

Arbitrage: The simultaneous buying and selling of two different but related securities, in one or more markets, in order to take advantage of the difference in price.

Asset Allocation: The transfer of investments into different categories in order to reduce risk and improve performance. The categories may include cash, bonds, or stocks devoted to specific sectors like industrials, gold, oil, real estate, or foreign stocks. Studies show that diversification can improve overall performance over a long period of time.

Balance Sheet: A statement of a company that shows its financial health as of a specific date.

Bar Chart: A chart used by technical analysts that presents a graphic display of the price actions of an investment. A vertical bar represents one day or time period and shows the high, low, close, and sometimes open prices. When one hundred or more bars are shown on a graphic with corresponding other data, a reasonable estimate of actions in the immediate future can be predicted to a modest level of confidence.

Bear Market: Long-term down trending market, usually lasting several quarters. There usually are three phases; distribution selling, panic selling, and capitulation. This is where the public finally gives up and liquidates. In the last phase, volume dries up. The bear market is over when PE ratios become traditional and a there is gradual increase in volume and price (not a spike).

Bell Curve: Sometimes called a bell shaped curve. It refers to the graphical representation of a statistical distribution of a typical population which looks like a church bell. Developed by Karl Gauss. Often called a Gaussian distribution curve.

Blue Chip Stocks: The high price stocks. Taken from the poker table where the blue chips are the most expensive. The higher prices come from long-term growth in earnings. The most valuable stocks.

Book Value: Equals total assets minus liabilities, minus intangible assets, minus stock issues ahead of common stock (preferred, convertibles). Then divide by the number of shares outstanding.

Bull Market: Long-term up trending market. Most of the time (but not always), there are three phases: accumulation, steady advance over a long period of time with increasing volume and prices, and ending with high activity and speculation by the general public. This last phase was described by Allan Greenspan as irrational exuberance. The Legends of Wall Street provide the maxim, "the dogs run before the crash".

Call Option: The right to purchase a specific number of shares of a specific stock at a specific price on or before the expiration date.

Capital Gain or Loss: The profit or loss due to sale of an asset. Long and short term have different tax rates which vary with politics.

Cash: Cash on hand plus short-term marketable securities that can be converted to cash on short notice.

Candlestick Chart: A short-term trading technique adapted from the Japanese traders of the 1700s. In addition to high and low, open and close of the bar charts, it shows the movement directions from open and close. Over fifty patterns were developed by the Eastern traders to detect price reversals. The difficulty in use comes from knowing when the patterns apply. The use of candlesticks is an art rather than a science.

Cash Flow: The company's net income useful for running the company. It is calculated by taking net income after taxes and adding depreciation, depletion, amortization, and certain other charges for tax purposes. If the reported profits exceed cash flow, someone is cooking the books.

Closed End Funds: An investment fund where the capitalization is fixed. No additional securities are added. The shares are trades in accordance with the laws of supply and demand.

Commodities: An economic product of agriculture or mining. Recently expanded to include energy products. A generic term to describe products where there is no franchise value.

Common Stock: Ownership in a company, divided into shares.

Correction: A minor change in a primary trend. In a bull market where the primary trend is up, a short-term downtrend is called a correction. In a bear market when the primary trend is down, a short-term uptrend is called a bear rally or bear trap

Current Asset: Cash or something that can be converted into cash within a year. Usually inventory and receivables are included.

Current Liability: Those financial obligations due within one year. Usually accounts payable, accrued expenses like labor and overhead, taxes, short-term notes, and short-term portion of long-term debt.

Current Ratio: Current assets divided by current liabilities. It is a quick look at the financial health of a company. It can vary between types of businesses, but usually about 2:1 for industrial companies.

Day Traders: Investors who trade several times per day and make a profit from the difference between the bid and asked prices of an auction market. An arbitrageur.

Debt Instruments: Contracts where a loan of money is made.

Depression: An extended period of retarded economic activity where unemployment increases.

Derivatives: A financial instrument where the value is dependent on the performance of another asset. One example is options on a stock which will appreciate if the price of the stock goes up.

Dilution: A reduction in the percentage of ownership represented by a share of stock by the issuance of additional shares at a reduced price. This occurs when a company issues many shares of stock (options) in lieu of wages to employees and does not account for them until they are exercised.

Diversification: Placing assets in different investments to spread out the risk. A key part of asset allocation.

Divergence: When indicators do not agree as to direction of a trend. This is used in technical analysis as a predictor of trend changes. Divergences eventually get resolved.

Dividend: The distribution of earnings by a company determined by the board of directors. May be in cash or stocks.

Dividend Yield: The yearly dividend amount divided by the price, expressed as a percentage.

Dogs: Usually low-priced stocks with little or no investment value. Dogs of the Dow would be the poorest performing of the Dow stocks.

Dollar Cost Averaging: Where the investor buys a fixed dollar amount of stock or fund each month. As the price fluctuates, the buyer gets more when the price is low and less when it is higher. Over a long period of time in a bull market, the average price will be lower.

Double bottom: A technical term to describe when a declining stock reached a previous low point. If it rebounds and does not go through the low point, it is considered a successful test, and is a signal for a change in trend and a strong upward movement. However, in a bear market, there can be triple bottoms. The price range of the double bottom becomes a support level.

Double Top: A technical term to describe when a rising stock reached a previous high point. If it does not go though and forms a double top, it signifies a change in trend and a strong movement downward. The price range of the double top becomes a resistance level.

Dow Jones Averages: There is the industrial average consisting of thirty stocks, the transportation average consisting of twenty stocks, and the utility average consisting of fifteen stocks. Together, the sixty-five stocks are called the composite average. Selected to represent the best-managed stocks as long-term investments.

Dow Theory: The first technical analysis widely used in the stock market. Uses averages to analyze market trends and uses one average to confirm another when the trend changes.

Due Diligence: The investigation of a security normally required by a person prior to investing.

Earnings Per Share: The net income after taxes divided by the number of shares.

Enterprise Value: The value of a company to its owners as a going concern.

Equity Investments: Where the investor owns a part of the investment property.

Fixed Assets: Land, buildings, equipment used by a company, and not a part of the product.

Franchise Value: The value added to a product line because of the loyalty of its customer base. Examples are Coca Cola, MacDonald's, and Gillette.

Fibonacci: A nickname given to Leonardo Pisano, a thirteenth-century mathematician noted for developing many advances in problem solving. The Fibonacci numbers are used in developing retracement analysis used in one branch of technical analysis.

Fiduciary: Person or entity that has a legal duty to act for another's benefit.

Fundamental Analysis: Analysis derived from earnings, revenue, growth, and evaluation of hard assets. It provides an assessment of the efficient use of capital, quality of company management, and the usefulness of the product or service to the market.

Futures Contract: A contract on a commodity bought for future acceptance or sold for future delivery. Used as a hedge against future price changes.

GAAP: Generally Accepted Accounting Practices. A standard method of accounting used for analysis of a company's financial statement.

Gaussian Distribution Curve: A normal to typical distribution curve used in statistical analysis. Developed by Karl Gauss. (See Bell Curve.)

Goodwill: A term to account for the difference between the value of an asset and the price paid. Also it refers to the intangible value of certain assets such as franchise value and patents.

Guru: A spiritual guide in Hinduism. A title often used for experts in stock analysis because the success of some of their predictions seem to require the intervention of the gods.

Income Statement: Also called the profit and loss statement. It reports the revenues and expenses of the company over the reporting period, usually a quarter or year.

Intangibles: Those items which are difficult to measure, such as goodwill, franchise value, and trademarks. The assignment of price is difficult and often arbitrary. This is an area where "cooking the books" is often done.

Intrinsic Value: The fundamental value of a company based on its ability to make profits.

Ishares: A series of closed end funds traded on the exchanges. They may be on certain sectors of the market.

Liquidation Value: The resulting value of the company if all its assets were sold and all the liabilities were paid off.

Liquidity: The amount or percentage of assets readily convertible into cash.

Management by Exception: A management technique whereby a well-defined plan is prepared and most of the management effort is concentrated on solving the exceptions to the plan. Works well with well thought out plans and requires much less management attention and cost. Poor planning results in difficult execution and added expenses.

Margin: The amount of cash needed to buy a stock. Currently it is a minimum of 50 percent.

Margin Call: The call by the broker to add cash to that account in order to maintain minimum margin.

Macroeconomics: The branch of economics that addresses the behavior of large economic entities such as countries and continents. It analyzes unemployment, gross domestic product, etc.

Market forces: Those forces that have an effect on the movement of the stock market. These include interest rates, taxes, education and skill of the work forces, information distribution, and transportation costs. May also include the local political and environmental attitude of the country.

Moving Average: A mathematical technique used in technical analysis to smooth data. At each time period an average is calculated from several data points and each new time period requires an old point to be removed when a new point is added.

NAIC: National Association of Investment Clubs. A non-profit largely volunteer organization dedicated to developing better investing skills of the club members through education.

Net Income: Income of a company after all expenses have been paid.

Operating Income: Income from operations after operating expenses have been paid.

Overbought: A term used to describe the overreaction of buyers when they have run the price up so the PE ratio is too high. One standard deviation above a typical price range for that stock.

Oversold: A term used to describe the overreaction of sellers when they have dropped the price so the PE ratio is too low. One standard deviation below a typical price range for that stock.

Passive Investor: One who oversees the investing process largely performed by others.

PE Ratio: The ratio of price divided by the net earnings. It is the benchmark of fundamental analysis. It can be reported for last year, the trailing twelve months, the current year, and the next year. Caution is urged to make sure of the time period used. This ratio helps in comparing return on investments for companies in different industries.

PEG ratio: The PE ratio divided by earnings growth. This is a better benchmark of fundamental analysis. Caution is urged to make sure of the time period used. Acceptable PEG ratios may vary with interest rates of the ten-year bond.

Portfolio: Total investment holdings.

Profit and Loss Statement: A company's income statement providing earnings for a specific time period. It is a primary indicator of the company's health.

Pro forma: To carry out in a perfunctory manner, or as a formality. It is an advanced statement submitted when all accurate information is not available. It is to be replaced at a later time.

Promissory Notes: A promise to pay the bearer or specific individual a fixed sum at a fixed time.

Put Options: The right to sell a specific number of shares of a specific stock at a specific price on or before the expiration date. It is the opposite of a call option and is used to hedge a position then spread the loss incase the stock drops.

Recession: A period of reduced economic activity, shorter than a depression.

REIT: Real Estate Investment trust. A REIT owns and operates income-producing real estate. Like most funds it is required to pay virtually all of its taxable income to its shareholders every year.

Resistance Levels: An upper level of a price range where supply increases to prevent further upward price movement. Breaking through a resistance level is a significant technical event.

Retained Earnings: The accumulated earnings of the corporation that has not been distributed.

Return on Invested Capital: Net income divided by total capital invested. The income may include interest, dividends, and capital appreciation.

Return on Equity: Net income divided by the total capital less loans outstanding on the asset.

Risk: The assessment of the probability of loss. Usually expressed in monetary terms.

Securities and Exchange Commission (SEC): A government agency formed in the 1930s depression with the responsibility to regulate the stock market. It requires reports from the companies that are available to the public.

SEC Reports: A form submitted to the Secretaries and Exchange Commission by publicly traded companies. 10K - Annual Report; 10Q Quarterly Report, others.

Selling Climax: A particularly high volume at the end of a fast and long decline in price which depletes the reserves of speculators. It has the appearance of panic selling. It usually marks the end of a correction, or the end of the second phase of a bear market.

Short Sale: A transaction where the sale takes place before the purchase. It is performed in the belief the stock price will deteriorate in the near future due to some particular weakness in the company. To accomplish the sale, the client's broker borrows the stock, which must be returned later. All dividends must be paid by the client (or borrower), to the lender, all during the time of the loan. It is a risky venture usually left to professionals. Very high short interest tends to predict future declines. However, liability is unlimited. The liability of a long position (owning the stock) is limited to the original investment. The liability of a short position is unlimited because the price could theoretically go to infinity.

Short Squeeze: When a stock with high short positions records some good news and the stock attracts a substantial number of new buyers. The rises in the stock forces several short sellers to get out of their position by buying back the stock. This buying added to the new buyers results in a rapid run up in price when the short sellers are squeezed out of their positions.

Split: Earnings Growth results in higher priced stock, which over time tends to price out many investors. In order to keep the price in the range of most investors, the shareholders vote to increase the number of shares into the same capitalization. The effect is to reduce the price and increase the number of shares in proportion. A person with one hundred shares of a $120 stock would end with two hundred shares of a $60 stock.

Strategy: A careful plan or method of accomplishing a given task. Achieving success by employing forces most efficiently.

Support Level: A lower level where demand increases to prevent further downward price movement. Breaking through a support level is a significant technical event.

Tactics: Operational techniques and maneuvers used to execute strategies.

Technical analysis:- The analysis derived from the price action of the stocks and indexes. Predictions are short term and the value of the prediction decays with time. It uses many indicators which include volume as well as price movement. Used primarily by short-term traders, but is useful for long-term investors to anticipate future adverse conditions in the company.

Transparency: The state of being transparent. In the stock market it refers to the ability to gather enough information to easily determine the financial health of a company. Opacity means the company is able to hide problems and present a false condition. The 1929 stock market crash was due in some measure to opacity. The Securities and Exchange Commission was formed in the mid-1930s to provide transparency to the investors. The U.S. has the most transparent stock market in the world.

Trend: The general direction of the movement of a stock or index. There are primary, secondary, and minor trends. The Dow Theory states that a major trend is presumed to continue until there is clear evidence of a reversal.

Volatility: The tendency for the price of a stock to move up or down; given as the percent movement over a period of time and based on price history. A volatility of .50 would mean the stock could move 50 percent over a given period of time. It is important to note that different elements of the market use different techniques to calculate volatility. Many professional traders use short periods like thirty days and long-term investors may use nine months.

Working Capital: Current assets minus current liabilities. A general indication of risk. Insufficient working capital indicates higher risk and lower profitability. Excess working capital indicates management cannot put the money to work efficiently in their primary business, or needs to hoard cash for some undetermined problem. It's related to current ratio.

Yield: The annual cash return divided by the investment. For bonds or debt instruments it's the interest rate, and for stocks or equity investments it's dividends.

SOURCES OF INFORMATION

Arie de Geus. *The Living Company*. Harvard Business Review. Vol. 75 No. 2. March/April 1997, pg. 51.

Barron's: 200 Liberty St., New York, NY 10281

CNBC TV. Financial News Channel on Cable Television

Business Week, McGraw Hill, 1221 Avenue of the Americas, New York, NY 10020

Durant, Will and Ariel *The Story Of Civilization*, 11 Volumes, New York, Simon and Schuster, 1935-1975

Edwards, Robert and John Magee. *Technical Analysis of Stock Trends*. 7th Edition. Boca Raton FL. CRC Press. 1997

Hirsch, Yale. *Stock Trader's Almanac*. 1982 Edition. Old Tappan NJ. Hirsch Organization Inc

Lowe, Janet. *Value Investing Made Easy*. New York, NY. McGraw-Hill 1996

Rukeyser, Louis. *Louis Rukeyser's Business Almanac*. New York, Simon and Schuster 1991

Rukeyser, Louis. *Wall Street Week*. Weekly Television Program

Trestor Kenneth R., *The Complete Options Player*. 3rd Edition, Lake Tahoe, NV. Institute for Options Research P.O. Box 6568 89449

Worden, Don. *Street-Smart Stock Reading*. Durham NC. Private papers, Worden Brothers Inc. 4905 Pine Cone Dr. Suites 10-12, Durham NC 27707

Worden, Don. *Traders Manifesto*. Durham NC. Private papers, Worden Brothers Inc. 4905 Pine Cone Dr. Suites 10-12, Durham NC 27707

AUTHOR BIOGRAPHY

Andy Karabinos began investing in stocks during the 1950s using methods taught by his parents. By 1987 he had accumulated a handsome portfolio. Anticipating a probable crash, he converted his portfolio into debt securities recommended by his broker. The resulting Enronesque debacle wiped out 95 percent of his total savings including his IRA. This book is a product of the lessons he learned.

0-595-23423-2

www.ingramcontent.com/pod-product-compliance
Lightning Source LLC
Chambersburg PA
CBHW030816180526
45163CB00003B/1307